Mercury Magic

How to Thrive During Retrogrades
and Tap Into the Power of the
Messenger Planet All Year Long

MARESSA BROWN

WORKMAN PUBLISHING
New York

Workman
Workman Publishing
Hachette Book Group, Inc.
1290 Avenue of the Americas
New York, NY 10104
workman.com

Workman is an imprint of Workman Publishing, a division of Hachette Book Group, Inc.
The Workman name and logo are registered trademarks of Hachette Book Group, Inc.

Design by Sarah Smith

The publisher is not responsible for websites (or their content)
that are not owned by the publisher.

Workman books may be purchased in bulk for business, educational,
or promotional use. For information, please contact your local bookseller or
the Hachette Book Group Special Markets Department at
special.markets@hbgusa.com.

Library of Congress Cataloging-in-Publication Data is available.

ISBN 978-1-5235-2406-8

First Edition July 2024

Printed in China on responsibly sourced paper.

10 9 8 7 6 5 4 3 2 1

To my husband, Kyle, whose natal Mercury in intuitive Cancer forms a harmonious sextile to my Virgo sun, supporting the most magical communication, understanding, and love.

CONTENTS

INTRODUCTION

In astrology, the sun can't help but be the (literal) star of the show. As it steadily charts its annual path from Aries through Pisces, spending about thirty days in each of the twelve signs, the blazing luminary guides us from one distinctive tone to the next. The sun sign you were born under also determines your response to the frequently asked question, "What sign are you?" (shorthand for "What sign was the sun in when you were born?"). While the sun offers insight into your self-image, identity, and confidence, it is just one integral detail of your astrological blueprint, aka your birth or natal chart. To better understand your thought processes and how you communicate, learn, absorb and share information, and engage with technology, look to the sun's closest neighbor: Mercury.

Envision a time in which you were completely in the zone while spilling your thoughts into a journal, making a presentation, or enjoying satisfying banter with a friend. Recall honing a new skill set or gaining knowledge, whether in a classroom or out in the world. In these cerebral moments, the celestial body running the show was Mercury, the planet of communication, transportation, and technology.

I've always felt especially connected to the messenger planet for good reason: Mercury is a major player in my birth chart. From the time I first learned how to write, I knew I was meant to spend my life doing exactly that. At age five, I asked my dad if he thought I would grow up to be an author, and he enthusiastically said yes. While he *is* an exceptionally doting father, his confidence in my ability to be a published author one day also stemmed from the fact that he understood my birth chart. I was born with not only the sun and moon but, importantly, Mercury in Virgo, the mutable earth sign known for being a pragmatic, detail-oriented bookworm. Because Virgo is ruled by the messenger planet, my parents anticipated that I'd fall head over heels for the written word. And given that I was born during a Mercury retrograde (something that's true for 25 percent of the population—more on this later!), it's no surprise that I'm compelled to write about, discuss, and defend the often-feared and misunderstood astrological event.

Knowing that Mercury has such a strong influence on my chart has empowered me to pursue my most ambitious goals, and I encourage everyone to explore Mercury in their own birth chart to better understand and leverage their communication style. Maybe you want to zero in on the best way to go to bat for a promotion or feel more at ease pouring your heart out to your BFF or significant other. Or perhaps you're hoping to chill out about and even benefit from Mercury's reversals, which happen three or four times a year. This book is meant to be a down-to-earth guide to tapping into the power of Mercury—during its backspins *and* all year round— and harnessing it to express yourself, connect with others, and even find the silver linings in its retrograde periods. Yes, really!

To start, you'll find a breakdown of astrology's basic building blocks, including what a natal chart looks like, how to find Mercury in yours, and other key symbols and definitions (like the elements and qualities) that will prove helpful as you read on. In Part One, you'll discover astrological must-knows about the messenger planet and how Mercury retrograde works, plus how you can thrive during these periods—especially in your career, in relationships, and in wellness. Part Two ushers you through transiting Mercury's "seasons" (aka its journey through each of the twelve sun signs), offering up tips for when it's direct, or moving forward, and tricks to call upon when it's retrograde. The book will also help you understand your natal Mercury, breaking down your superpowers, challenges, and compatibility with other signs as well as your Mercury house placement, which tells you where in life your unique communication abilities play out.

Some notes to consider as you move through the book:

Mercury—in your chart and in the sky—is just one piece of a complex puzzle. While you may have been born with Mercury in gregarious, outgoing fire sign Sagittarius, it's possible that your sun is in private, aloof water sign Scorpio, which may mean you're not as direct and boisterous as, say, someone born with *both* the sun and Mercury in Sag. Or maybe your Mercury is in peace-loving air sign Libra, but at the time of your birth, it was clashing with go-getter Mars, which may nudge you to be more comfortable with passionate debate than the average person who has Mercury in the sign of the Scales.

Similarly, you might find that Mercury is currently moving through a generally laid-back sign like Taurus, but it's interacting with another planet in the sky or your chart in a surprisingly excitable, breakthrough-bringing way. In other words, contradictions are inevitable in astrology, which is complex and multidimensional—just like us and our daily lives.

You can use astrology to learn about yourself as well as other people. Two of the best gifts astrology has to offer are bolstered self-awareness—something you'll absolutely get out of studying your natal Mercury—and an understanding of and compassion for others. To that end, I encourage you to explore this book with a dear friend, significant other, or family member. Maybe even read it with someone you often butt heads with. My hope is you'll find helpful hints that can preempt crossed wires.

The goal of this book is to help you feel informed, empowered, and seen. More often than not, Mercury is associated with its retrogrades and has a reputation for being the culprit of complete havoc. Sure, one of its nicknames is "the trickster planet," but it is also the celestial body that fuels your thoughts and ability to bring them into the world. By becoming more familiar with Mercury, you can easily tackle unfounded fearmongering head-on and share what's on your mind with more conviction and confidence.

ASTROLOGY BASICS

Imagine a time when you stood under a dark sky splattered with shimmering stars, many of them banding together to cut patterns into the canvas of nighttime. Or maybe you were taken aback by the dramatic sight of a luminous full moon as you stood on a beach and noticed its obvious influence on the tides. Moments like these can't help but remind us that we're connected to the heavenly bodies above and surrounding us.

Perhaps you picked up this book hoping to learn more about your personal astrology or wanting to understand how the planets' everyday movements are, like the weather, setting a particular tone and laying the groundwork for various events to transpire. Either way, a wonderful place to start is by learning more about the luminaries (aka the sun and the moon) and the planets, each overseeing specific areas of life and possessing unique characteristics and powers.

You'll also do well to consider the additional essential details (see page 16) that will support exploration of your birth chart, astrological transits, and, specifically, Mercury. Because these key building blocks come together to tell a complex story about your perspective, interests, strengths, challenges, and even your life path, they're worth discovering and holding in mind as you dive deeper into astrology.

The Luminaries and the Planets

Although zeroing in on Mercury can offer especially valuable intel on your communication style, all of the luminaries and planets (aka natal placements) in your birth chart work in tandem to help shape your personality, point of view, and life story. That means you'll do well to consider the influence of each.

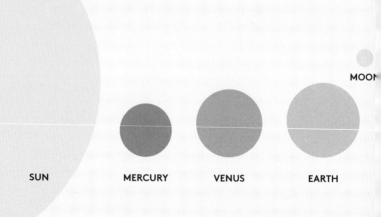

SUN   MERCURY   VENUS   EARTH   MOON

THE SUN ☉

The blazing star that serves as the center of our solar system colors your:

* Core identity
* Self-image
* Confidence
* Expression of pride
* Self-esteem
* Purpose

THE MOON ☽

The moon is what I like to call your astrological "emotional compass," helping to shape your:

* Inner world
* Emotional nature and needs
* Intuition and instincts
* Sense of security
* Nurturing style and the ways you want to be nurtured

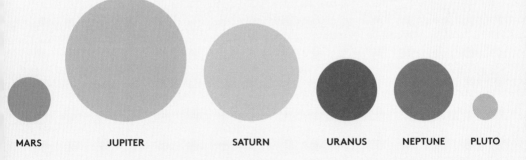

MARS   JUPITER   SATURN   URANUS   NEPTUNE   PLUTO

MERCURY ☿

The messenger planet
(and speediest celestial body)
informs your:

* Communication style
* Approach to information-gathering and sharing
* Thought processes
* Decision making
* Ideal strategies for learning

VENUS ♀

The planet of romance and
values influences your:

* Creative self-expression
* Perception of beauty
* Relationship to earning money
* Experience of pleasure
* Demonstration of affection

MARS ♂

The go-getter planet,
which fuels passion and
dynamism, powers your:

* Action style
* Inner drive
* Anger
* Motivation
* Self-assertion

JUPITER ♃

The largest planet in our solar
system, which has a magnifying
effect, impacts your:

* Experience of attracting and making your own luck
* Self-expression of generosity
* Thirst for seeking out and soaking up wisdom
* Interactions with opportunities
* Faith in others

SATURN ♄

The taskmaster planet, which oversees rules and reality checks, informs your:

* Approach to setting boundaries
* Life lessons related to discipline
* Fears (and restrictions that may stem from them)
* Approach to responsibility
* Relationship to authority figures

URANUS ♅

The game-changing planet, which often spurs breakthroughs and shake-ups, affects your:

* Approach to innovation
* Rebellion against rules or convention
* Expression of individuality
* Experience of personal freedom
* Relationship to limits and boundaries

NEPTUNE ♆

The mystical planet, which tends to cloud rational thought, helps to shape your:

* Imagination and creativity
* Experience of spirituality
* Desire to heal and care for others
* Intuitive and psychic abilities
* Relationship to dreams

PLUTO ♀

The planet of regeneration, which is connected to the subconscious, guides your:

* Experience of infatuation and obsessions
* Approach to uncovering the hidden truth of any situation
* Desire to find deeper meaning
* Approach to transformation
* Relationship to power struggles and control

What It Means When a Planet Is "in" a Sign

Unlike astronomy, which studies the stars' movement in real time, Western astrology utilizes a fixed system called the tropical zodiac, which aligns the spring equinox with the first degree of Aries, the first zodiac sign. At the core of this system is the sun's apparent path across the ecliptic: the circle of twelve fixed constellations that surround the Earth. Here's a simple way to think about this: Envision yourself standing in the middle of a 360-degree circular room, and painted on the walls around you are all twelve constellations, or zodiac signs, each of which spans 30 degrees. The sun, the moon, and all the planets are projected over the constellations. Although Earth moves around the sun, it appears from our perspective that the sun, the moon, and all the planets are moving around *us*, making their way across the ecliptic. And the tropical zodiac is based on our earthly view. So, the sign that a planet occupies is determined by our vantage point—how each constellation appears from where we're standing on Earth. It also hinges on our experience of the seasons, as a new cycle always kicks off with the spring equinox, which is when the sun moves into the first sign of the zodiac, Aries.

Because each celestial body moves at a different rate and in its own pattern across the ecliptic, each will be "in" a sign for a varied amount of time. The sun, for instance, spends about thirty days in a sign. Meanwhile, Mercury spends anywhere from fifteen to sixty days in a sign. As the celestial bodies make their way through the twelve signs, they form harmonizing or tense angles with one another, fueling the astrological weather of the moment, which we all experience collectively.

At the same time, they connect with the placements of the sun, moon, and planets in your birth chart (more on that in a moment), making for both joy-filled days and challenging moments. For example, if you were born when the sun was in intuitive Pisces, and tomorrow, the moon happens to be in fellow emotionally intelligent water sign Cancer, you'll be feeling more balanced, tranquil, and peaceful. But while Mars, the planet of action and aggression, is in Virgo, which is the opposite of Pisces, you might find conflicts arise more frequently, especially within one-on-one relationships.

Transiting vs. Natal

Throughout the book, you'll see references to "transiting Mercury," which refers to the planet as it moves through the signs in real time. We'll also talk about "natal Mercury," which is your Mercury sign—think of it as a screenshot of what transiting Mercury was up to (for instance, the sign it was in and the other planets it was interacting with) at the exact moment you were born.

The Birth Chart:
Your Astrological Blueprint

When you're trading personal details with a potential partner, a new colleague, or a casual acquaintance, a quick and easy way to understand their basic disposition—and perhaps also your compatibility—is to ask, "What's your sign?" While learning someone's sun sign can be a wonderful jumping-off point to get to know them, it's just the tip of the iceberg when it comes to their unique astrological picture.

Everyone has a distinctive natal chart—aka birth chart—based on their exact birthdate (including the year), birth time, and birthplace. This chart denotes not only which sign the sun was moving through when they were born but also the placement of the moon and planets—including Mercury—at the precise time of their birth from the vantage point of their birthplace. Because the sun, the moon, and the planets all move at different speeds, it's common to have been born with the sun in, say, Leo, but the moon in a completely different sign like, say, Capricorn, and Venus in Cancer. Each of these natal placements can offer valuable insight into your motivations, perspective, personality, strengths, and opportunities for growth.

Western astrology may be more than 2,000 years old, but thanks to a recent revival of enthusiasm for the practice, it's become more common to know your astrological "big three," which are your sun sign, moon sign, and rising sign (aka ascendant). If you've gone a bit further, you might know your "big six": sun, moon, and rising as well as your Mercury, Venus, and Mars signs.

While this book will help you get familiar with your natal Mercury so you can be an even more self-assured and effective communicator, I advocate doing a deep dive on each of these placements—and really, your entire birth chart—to foster self-awareness.

How to Cast Your Chart

For starters, you'll need your birth month, date, and year; time of birth; and place of birth, including city, state or province, and country. This info is usually included on a long-form birth certificate. If you don't have it on hand, you can request it from the county where you were born. From there, you can:

* Visit my website, maressabrown.com, where you can generate a free natal chart.

* Use the Time Passages app or a paid software that professional astrologers use, like Solar Fire (for PCs and Macs) or Astro Gold (for Macs).

* Work one-on-one with a professional astrologer. Many astrologers offer birth chart readings.

Throughout the book, you'll learn how to interpret key details in your birth chart, especially those related to your natal Mercury. You'll also find more resources for understanding your astrological blueprint on page 163.

For an example of a birth chart in general—and one in which Mercury's strengths are spotlit—check out the opposite page. Amanda Gorman, inaugural poet and the first person to be named National Youth Poet Laureate, has a noticeable Mercury influence in her birth chart. Because her rising sign is Mercury-ruled earth sign Virgo, her chart is ruled by the messenger planet. Her natal Mercury is in Pisces, sitting at 29 degrees (the final degree of a sign, aka the anaretic degree). This placement signifies that the messenger planet's powers are intensified and associated with a fated mission. Gorman was born to harness thoughts and language (Mercury) to convey dreams and emotion (Pisces). With Mercury in her seventh house of partnership, collaboration comes naturally to Gorman, and because it is conjunct action-oriented Mars, the way she communicates is tightly tied to how she takes action. This reflects the way she uses her writing as a form of activism.

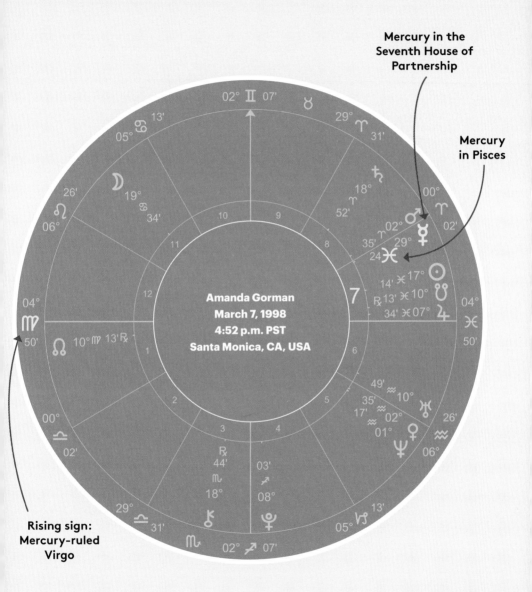

Mercury in the
Seventh House of
Partnership

Mercury
in Pisces

02° ♊ 07' ♉

13' 29° ♈

05° ♋ 31'

26' ♌ 19° ♋ 34' 18° ♄ 52' 00° ♈ 02'

06° 02° ♂ ♈
35' ♐ 29° ♈
24 ♓

10 9 8

11

12 7 14' ♓ 17° ☉
R 13' ♓ 10° ☊
34' ♓ 07' ♃

04° ♍ 50' 1 04° ♓
50'

Amanda Gorman
March 7, 1998
4:52 p.m. PST
Santa Monica, CA, USA

♌ 10° ♍ 13' R♃ 6

2

00° ♎ 3 4 5 49' ♒ 10°
02' 35' ♒
17' ♒ 02° ♇ 26°
01° ♒
06° ♒

R 44' ♏ 18° 03' 08° ♐

29° ♎ 31' ♏ 05° ♑ 13'

02° ♐ 07'

Rising sign:
Mercury-ruled
Virgo

Essential Details

As you explore astrology, keep these must-knows in mind.

THE RULING PLANETS

Every sign has a planetary ruler that influences how it expresses itself. For instance, if your Mercury is in Cancer, the moon's intuitive, emotional energy informs your communication style.

- Aries: Mars
- Taurus: Venus
- Gemini: Mercury
- Cancer: The moon
- Leo: The sun
- Virgo: Mercury
- Libra: Venus
- Scorpio: Pluto (modern ruler), Mars (traditional ruler)*
- Sagittarius: Jupiter
- Capricorn: Saturn
- Aquarius: Uranus (modern ruler), Saturn (traditional ruler)*
- Pisces: Neptune (modern ruler), Jupiter (traditional ruler)*

*Prior to the discovery of the outer planets (Neptune, Uranus, and Pluto), traditional astrologers only referred to the inner planets (Mars, Venus, Mercury, Jupiter, and Saturn, plus the sun and the moon) as rulers of the twelve signs. Once the outer planets were discovered, modern astrologers incorporated them as new or corulers of several signs (Scorpio, Aquarius, and Pisces). Both traditional and modern rulers illustrate the signs' characteristics.

THE ELEMENTS

The twelve signs are divided into four elements—fire, earth, air, and water—each of which has its own signature traits. When exploring Mercury (either transiting or natal), you'll want to think about how the elements function to get a sense of how the messenger planet will express itself. If it's moving through a fire sign, we'll all be inclined toward passionate self-expression. And if it was in an earth sign when you were born, your communication style tends to be grounded and pragmatic.

 FIRE

Aries, Leo, Sagittarius

Driven, adventurous, action-oriented, and dynamic

 EARTH

Taurus, Virgo, Capricorn

Practical, rational, analytical, and organized

 AIR

Gemini, Libra, Aquarius

Information-seeking, social, unattached, and cerebral

 WATER

Cancer, Scorpio, Pisces

Artistic, intuitive, sensitive, and empathic

THE QUALITIES

Within each element, there's one of each quality (also referred to as "modality" or "triplicity"): cardinal, fixed, and mutable. Each speaks to the innate temperament of a sign.

 ## CARDINAL

These signs excel at taking initiative and visionary thinking but might struggle to get to the finish line.

 ## FIXED

These signs commit to concrete plans and see them through but also dig their heels in.

 ## MUTABLE

These signs are open-minded, experimental, and receptive but have trouble taking a stand.

Spring

Aries (cardinal)

Taurus (fixed)

Gemini (mutable)

Summer

Cancer (cardinal)

Leo (fixed)

Virgo (mutable)

Fall

Libra (cardinal)

Scorpio (fixed)

Sagittarius (mutable)

Winter

Capricorn (cardinal)

Aquarius (fixed)

Pisces (mutable)

THE ASPECTS

Planetary aspects describe how the transiting sun, moon, or planets or natal placements are interacting with one another, based on the distance between them.

 ## CONJUNCTION

Two celestial bodies are in the same spot, which means they're functioning in sync.

 ## OPPOSITION

Placements that are 180 degrees apart are at odds with one another but may offer an opportunity for growth.

 ## QUINCUNX

Placements that are 150 degrees apart may contradict one another and require holding space for two energies that are truly dissimilar.

 ## TRINE

Placements that are 120 degrees apart indicate an easygoing harmony between them.

 ## SQUARE

Placements that are 90 degrees apart spur tension but can bring about productive change or action.

 ## SEXTILE

Placements that are 60 degrees apart set an easygoing vibe and present an invitation or opportunity to harness their powers.

 ## SEMI-SEXTILE

Placements that are 30 degrees apart set the stage for disharmony but can work when each one's unique strengths have a chance to shine.

THE HOUSES

Every birth chart is split into twelve pie slices referred to as houses. Think of your natal chart's houses as a map of the stars and planets specific to when and where you were born. The top of the chart (houses seven through twelve) shows the signs that were visible in the night sky at the exact time of your birth from your vantage point on Earth. The bottom of the chart (houses one through six) are the signs that could be seen from the opposite hemisphere. And as the Earth rotates on its axis over the course of twenty-four hours, the sun, the moon, Mercury, and all the other planets appear to parade clockwise through the houses. They all rise over the eastern horizon, the same spot the sun rises over. On every natal chart, the eastern horizon is represented by the cusp of the first house—aka the ascendant or rising sign. If you were born midday, the sun and planets that travel closely to it, such as Mercury, were high in the sky above you, at the top of the chart (the tenth house). They set in the west (the angle that sits opposite the ascendant, known as the descendant), so if you were born when it was nighttime in your hemisphere, they'll appear at the bottom of the chart.

Each of the twelve houses represents a specific area of life and is associated with a planet (referred to as the natural planetary ruler) as well as one of the twelve signs, meaning their energies match. You'll notice that each house in your chart is associated with a sign that is likely *different* from the sign that's generally tied to that house. The signs linked to your houses are based on your ascendant and are part of what make your chart distinctly your own.

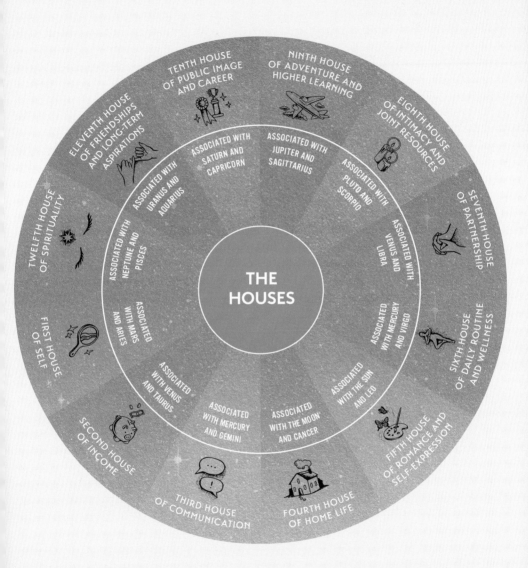

THE HOUSES

TENTH HOUSE OF PUBLIC IMAGE AND CAREER

NINTH HOUSE OF ADVENTURE AND HIGHER LEARNING

ELEVENTH HOUSE OF FRIENDSHIPS AND LONG-TERM ASPIRATIONS

EIGHTH HOUSE OF INTIMACY AND JOINT RESOURCES

TWELFTH HOUSE OF SPIRITUALITY

SEVENTH HOUSE OF PARTNERSHIP

FIRST HOUSE OF SELF

SIXTH HOUSE OF DAILY ROUTINE AND WELLNESS

SECOND HOUSE OF INCOME

FIFTH HOUSE OF ROMANCE AND SELF-EXPRESSION

THIRD HOUSE OF COMMUNICATION

FOURTH HOUSE OF HOME LIFE

ASSOCIATED WITH SATURN AND CAPRICORN

ASSOCIATED WITH JUPITER AND SAGITTARIUS

ASSOCIATED WITH URANUS AND AQUARIUS

ASSOCIATED WITH PLUTO AND SCORPIO

ASSOCIATED WITH NEPTUNE AND PISCES

ASSOCIATED WITH VENUS AND LIBRA

ASSOCIATED WITH MARS AND ARIES

ASSOCIATED WITH MERCURY AND VIRGO

ASSOCIATED WITH VENUS AND TAURUS

ASSOCIATED WITH THE SUN AND LEO

ASSOCIATED WITH MERCURY AND GEMINI

ASSOCIATED WITH THE MOON AND CANCER

When you're first learning about the building blocks of natal astrology, it's not uncommon to feel slightly overwhelmed. Going beyond your sun sign and diving into all the intricate and nuanced specifics of a birth chart can be daunting. But as you discover more about astrology (something even seasoned astrology students and professionals do perpetually), having a solid understanding of these details will only enhance your ability to connect the dots between astrological concepts, amplifying your self-awareness.

For instance, the ruling planets can offer an extra layer of insight into your communication style. If your Mercury is ruled by Mars, the planet of action, you can be better aware of your superpowers (being direct and passionate) and challenges (tending toward argumentativeness). By considering the elements, you'll learn that if you have Mercury in a deeply intuitive water sign, you possess innate emotional intelligence. Once you're familiar with the qualities, you'll see that should your Mercury fall in a fixed sign, you'll do well to foster adaptability and self-compassion when you find yourself struggling to pivot to a different mindset or approach. Bearing the aspects in mind, you'll be able to note that perhaps your Mercury forms a conjunction to your natal Saturn, indicating that you think and express yourself in a serious, self-disciplined way. And pinpointing which house your natal Mercury lives in will equip you with an empowering sense of the areas of life in which you excel at communication and information gathering.

As you move through the rest of the book and read about transiting Mercury, your natal Mercury, and your Mercury house placement, I invite you to refer back to this section whenever you need a refresher on the essential details. Recognizing how they interplay with the planet of communication—whether in your birth chart or as Mercury travels across the ecliptic—can help you stand even more strongly in your sense of self while strengthening your connections with others.

PART ONE

Mercury on the Move

Some planets, like Uranus, Neptune, and Pluto, travel through the zodiac slowly, spending years in a particular sign. In turn, they take just as long to make their mark. Meanwhile, the faster-moving planets deliver life's twists and turns on a day-to-day basis. So it's no surprise that we feel the effects of the speediest planet in the solar system intensely. That celestial body is none other than Mercury.

Mercury completes one orbit of the sun every eighty-eight Earth days, traveling at an average speed of roughly 107,000 miles per hour. It also happens to be the planet closest to the sun, which means they either occupy the same sign at the same time or Mercury is in the sign immediately preceding or following the sign the sun is in. The reason this fast-paced planet might fall behind the sun? Three or four times a year, for about three weeks at a time, Mercury slows down and goes retrograde, appearing to move backward through the zodiac (we'll dive into this later in Part One—see page 28).

Whether it is cruising full-speed ahead or slowly backing up, Mercury's journey directly influences how we connect with others, get from point A to point B, interact with technology, and share and receive information. During its time in an emotional water sign, you'll be more apt to check with your heart rather than your head before deciding how to address an ongoing issue with a loved one. And when it's in a cerebral, social air sign, it's easier to think more rationally. You'll also find you can more readily make and keep plans with friends. While the communication planet is more effective when it is in certain signs (like the ones it rules: Gemini and Virgo), there are ways to take advantage of its trip through any sign.

Mercury Must-Knows

* Named after the Roman deity who served as the messenger of the gods and was associated with speed and trade

* Nicknames: The messenger planet and the trickster planet

* Rules communication, transportation, and technology

* Rules Gemini, the mutable air sign, and Virgo, the mutable earth sign

* Associated with the Third House of Communication, the section of an astrological chart that's devoted to speaking, learning, mental connections, siblings, and neighbors

* Associated with the Sixth House of Wellness, the section of an astrological chart that involves daily routine, health, everyday work, and pets

Mercury's Trip
Across the Ecliptic

As Mercury makes its way through the zodiac, its meetups and conflicts with other celestial bodies will affect self-expression and idea generation. Say Mercury is hanging out at 15° Taurus with Jupiter, which has a magnifying effect on everything it encounters. They'll form a conjunction, meaning they're meeting up at the same degrees of a particular sign, which can set the stage for over-the-top communication, open-mindedness, and optimistic thinking. A more tense—but also activating—connection between celestial bodies is the square, which happens when one planet sits 90 degrees away from the other. On a day during which Mercury squares Uranus, everyone's more likely to experience out-of-the-blue shake-ups. Cue a surge of frenetic, nervous energy, which can make for sudden accidents, technological glitches, or shocking news. On the bright side, Mercury squaring Uranus can fire up thrilling breakthroughs and original thinking.

Simultaneously, Mercury could connect with a significant point in your birth chart, affecting your mental energy and communication. These transits usually last about a day but can be repeated weeks later if Mercury goes retrograde and retraces its path over that point in your birth chart. For example, when Mercury lands on (aka conjuncts) your sun (which oversees identity), you'll be more confident, self-assured, and centered in how you present thoughts and ideas because Mercury's setting a cerebral tone that's aligned with your self-image.

Mercury Retrograde, Demystified

If you've ever felt like a Mercury retrograde literally just ended before another seemingly began, that's because the astrological event happens almost seasonally—a result of Mercury's fast pace. More often than not, Mercury zips ahead through the zodiac, moving from one sign to the next. This is referred to as "Mercury direct." But every three or four months, the messenger planet's pace slows to nearly a full pause before appearing to move backward through the signs from our vantage point here on Earth. This is called "Mercury retrograde."

In addition to the retrograde itself, there are a couple other must-know periods leading up to and following the astrological event.

Other Planets' Retrogrades

Chances are when you hear the word "retrograde," you automatically think of Mercury. That's likely because it's the planet that goes retrograde most frequently, as it's the fastest-moving celestial body. Nonetheless, every planet in the solar system (save the luminaries, the sun and the moon) takes its turn retrograding, urging slowdowns and self-reflection related to its distinctive themes. Here's how often you can expect each to move backward and for how long.

♀ **Venus:** Every 18 months for 6 weeks

♂ **Mars:** Every 2 years for 2 to 2.5 months

♃ **Jupiter:** Once a year for about 4 months

♄ **Saturn:** Once a year for about 4.5 months

♅ **Uranus:** Once a year for about 5 months

♆ **Neptune:** Once a year for 5 to 6 months

♇ **Pluto:** Once a year for 5 to 6 months

The Pre- and Post-Shadows

Well before Mercury is technically retrograde and even after the transit has officially ended, you might find it's more challenging to get your point across with a higher-up or that a long-awaited email inexplicably doesn't make it to your inbox. What you're experiencing are the pre- and post-shadow periods of the retrograde. Basically, Mercury takes a couple of weeks to slow down ahead of its retrograde as well as a couple of weeks to ramp back up to full speed after it turns direct. As Mercury's speed is reduced, the areas of life it oversees—communication, transportation, and technology—simply won't function as smoothly and efficiently as usual.

During the pre-shadow, you might get sneak peeks of themes and lessons that will come up for you during the official retrograde phase. At this time, Mercury is still moving forward, albeit slowly, over particular degrees of a sign. When Mercury's retrograde, it'll go back over those same degrees, creating an opportunity to redo, edit, or reimagine something that's happening in that area of your natal chart. Say that during the pre-shadow, Mercury moves ahead between 7° and 21° Leo, which fall in your sixth house of wellness. Perhaps it's time to reassess how much you're spending on that group fitness membership if you're not going as regularly as you planned, or you're realizing that the flex schedule you set with your boss a while back needs to be revised so you can meet certain responsibilities at home.

During the post-shadow, Mercury, direct once more, will pass through that same point in the sky a third time, during which you can truly move forward with whatever you reenvisioned during the retrograde. You'll also have the chance to debrief reflections and emotions that arose as well as ensure old business has been fully tended to and zhuzh any plans you want to put in motion.

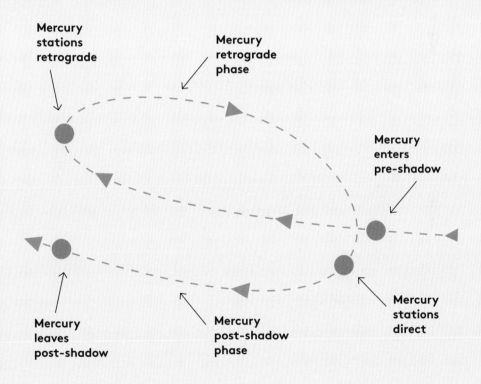

Mercury
stations
retrograde

Mercury
retrograde
phase

Mercury
enters
pre-shadow

Mercury
stations
direct

Mercury
leaves
post-shadow

Mercury
post-shadow
phase

The Mercury Storm

For several days leading up to and following a retrograde's kickoff and completion, slowdowns and delays are particularly likely because Mercury is in its "storm period," which means it's moving at its absolute slowest. Although Mercury isn't technically retrograde just yet—or anymore—it's still best to proceed with caution when pushing forward on new projects during the storm.

The Most Intense Days of Any Mercury Retrograde

The day that Mercury goes—aka stations—retrograde, it comes to almost a complete halt. The same is true of the day it stations direct. It's on these days that you may especially feel those stereotypical effects of a Mercury retrograde. Communication gets scrambled, transportation is chaotic, and technology goes haywire. While these occurrences can catch you off guard and often set a tone that's unsettling, irritating, frustrating, or extremely frenetic, it's important to remember that this isn't illustrative of the entire three-week retrograde period. It's just that Mercury tends to wreak the most havoc on the days it stations.

What You Can Expect During Mercury Retrograde

The pressure to be scheduled every minute of the day, to accomplish, to achieve, and to always keep your foot on the gas lest you appear unproductive has likely never been more pervasive. It's pretty much impossible to go through a typical day and not feel like—at least at some point, if not perpetually—you're drowning in an avalanche of electronic alerts and notifications. Hustle culture is toxic and draining us all. But it's also why I suspect even the biggest astrology skeptics admit there's something to Mercury retrograde. Because we're so attached to productivity, connected to technology, and compelled to be mentally engaged with others, it's no wonder we're all feeling the planet of communication's backward spins more than ever.

If you've heard anything at all about Mercury retrograde, it's that the three-week period causes all hell to break loose. You've no doubt heard a friend blame their latest breakup or most recent work drama on Mercury-induced chaos. And while miscommunications and delays spurred by Mercury retrograde might very well contribute to incidents like these, it really isn't fair to paint the transit with such a broad—and negative—brush. Its effects are a lot more nuanced.

A few things you can almost guarantee will occur when Mercury is retrograde:

You'll be pulled backward. Just like the planet of communication appears to retrace its path in the sky, you'll feel tugged back in time. Sometimes this manifests as a sudden desire to finally unpack and reorganize belongings that have been collecting dust in an attic or hallway closet or to go through a box of photographs that haven't seen the light of day for decades. It could be that you'll have to tend to unfinished business—or even business you thought was finished but now requires revision.

What's past is present. Your best friend from college who you haven't talked to in a decade suddenly DMs you and wants to catch up over coffee because they just happen to be in town. A former colleague wants to discuss potentially working together on a project they're helming. And yes, this effect of Mercury retrograde might also lead to an ex or a date who ghosted you texting out of the blue. Pro tip: While some blasts from a past life might be opportunities to rewrite history, others actually don't carry as much weight as you might think. Remember, Mercury is the trickster planet, so not every communication you receive during retrograde is meant to be engaged with. In fact, the purpose for some of these incidents is to gauge your growth.

Projects you had no choice but to start during a previous retrograde pick back up. Ever have a project, task, or chore seem to take an abnormally long time to complete? Sure, in some cases, this might be because you—or someone else involved—is a terrible procrastinator. But it's also possible that you originally dove in when Mercury was retrograde, so of course progress crept along at a snail's pace. The best time for you to revisit and/or complete the project is when Mercury is in the same exact state that it was when the undertaking was initiated.

For example, I've found that a bill for a doctor's appointment I had during a retrograde might not show up until the next retrograde phase—or even several later. And because I was so eager to start designing my ketubah (Jewish wedding contract), I began the conversation with an Etsy seller two days before Mercury went direct. It took several months—all the way until the very beginning of the next Mercury retrograde phase—for us to finalize and approve it for printing.

Your impulse to slow down and go inward will skyrocket.
Mercury rules our mental energy and thought processes. When the messenger planet moves forward, we're more likely to share, write, speak, and connect with the world around us. But its retrograde periods set a quieter, more introspective tone. For three weeks, you could feel more meditative, mindful, self-reflective—but also be in your head more than usual and possibly even find it tougher to express yourself. The solution is often to pivot away from the external and focus on inner work (think journaling, meditating). Of course, inner work is sometimes best accomplished with a little help from a therapist, mentor, life coach, or even a spiritual leader.

Technology glitches and transportation conundrums ensue.
Mercury retrogrades are notorious for wreaking havoc on tech and turning your regular headache of a commute into an utter nightmare. I can't even begin to tell you how many times I've had

to be bailed out of locking my keys in the car, a flat tire, or a dead battery—all during Mercury retrograde. You may find yourself wondering why on earth you thought you could rely on your fitness tracker to store valuable medical info or your laptop to save the deck you need for that key presentation. Even if you're not internally (or maybe externally) screaming over files that have gone missing, an out-of-warranty device that's refusing to hold a charge, or emails that make zero sense, Mercury retrograde's hallmark glitches can curb your best efforts to check to-dos off your list. Even the speediest Wi-Fi will creep along à la 1995 dial-up, and you'll inexplicably be caught in bumper-to-bumper traffic outside of rush hour. These incidents don't happen every single day for three weeks, but they're more likely to occur when Mercury's moving backward and can serve as a reminder that this period is conducive to taking your time versus plowing ahead.

How to ~~Survive~~ **THRIVE** During Mercury Retrograde

Despite the challenges it can lead to, Mercury retrograde's bad reputation is thoroughly exaggerated; it's not going to upend everything you've been striving for, and it's probably not the sole culprit of every roadblock you encounter. Just like any other astrological event, Mercury retrograde is neither 100 percent positive nor 100 percent negative. It actually features as many opportunities as it does challenges, which means it *is* possible to not only survive but thrive during Mercury's backspins. Read on for how to make the most of them.

Find conscious ways to slow down physically. Some of us excel at chilling out while others struggle with it. But Mercury retrogrades nudge all of us to pinpoint and then prioritize activities that support mindfulness, being present, and taking a step back from the hustle of everyday life. Maybe for you that's spending time at a day spa, going on a leisurely hike, or taking a swim. Any pastime that nurtures your parasympathetic nervous system and soothes your mind is worth exploring and can help you feel more centered when stereotypical Mercury retrograde obstacles, such as delays or misunderstandings, are threatening to get the best of you.

Spend time on activities that involve looking in the rearview.
Consider scrapbooking, catching up with an old friend, or re-creating a cherished memory with your college crew, all of which can serve as valuable, emotionally centering reminders of where you've been and how far you've come. Antiquing, thrifting, or exploring a natural history or art museum you haven't visited in years can inspire an appreciation for the past. You might also declutter old clothes, tchotchkes, or keepsakes that no longer serve you. Reorganization can help you create more physical space and feel refreshing.

Reframe this time as an opportunity for self-work. When any planet is retrograde, we're encouraged to go inward to explore its themes. Because Mercury rules not only speaking but listening, too, its retrogrades present a chance to reflect on your thought patterns and how you're receiving information. Doing so may boost your self-awareness around anything from relationship dynamics to joint finances to long-term aspirations. The area of life that you'll feel urged to explore during a particular Mercury retrograde will depend on which house in your natal chart the communication planet is moving backward through—see page 88.

Set your expectations accordingly. Being aware that Mercury is retrograde during any situation that's heavy on communication, transportation, and/or technology can help you manage your time and plan differently from how you would if Mercury was direct. Whether you're headed to a job interview or a movie, give yourself plenty of extra time—and then some. And when a wrench gets thrown in that seemingly perfect plan . . .

Do your best to meet confusion and delays with a sense of humor. There will definitely be times when you're in the midst of a total retrograde nightmare that deserves nothing less than a full-on freakout. But for the most part, Mercury, the trickster planet that it is, causes disorder that is irritating and short-lived rather than drama that'll truly turn your life upside down. That said, when Mercury setbacks strike, it'll ultimately serve you best to take a deep breath and try to find an aspect of the situation you can laugh about.

Thriving at Work

Because most of us depend heavily on technology, seemingly endless communication, and transportation to accomplish our professional to-dos, work is where you often can't help but notice retrograde-induced chaos unfolding—perhaps more than any other area of life. That said, there are plenty of ways you can simultaneously minimize Mercury meltdowns and take advantage of the transit in your professional life.

Refresh your résumé and professional profiles. With Mercury moving backward three to four times a year, not every retrograde phase will inspire you to freshen up your social presence, add new qualifications to your résumé, or flirt with a different font or headshot on your website, but it can be an opportune time to take any or all of those actions. Slowing your usual hustle to examine how you're presenting yourself professionally can set you up for advancement once Mercury's direct.

Revisit and reconnect. Maybe you were offered a side hustle that you didn't have time for several months ago, but now it would fit in nicely with your current projects. Or perhaps you've been wanting to reconnect with an old coworker who might be able to refer you for an intriguing opportunity. Mercury retrograde is your cue to reach back out, retrace your steps, and explore whether a conversation from the past has potential to be continued in the present.

Get intentional. From vision boarding to journaling, you can make the most of the self-reflective tone that Mercury retrograde sets by devoting quality time to exploring what you want to accomplish in the coming months. And while you're at it, don't forget to give yourself plenty of credit for how far you've come already.

Schedule a review. It may just so happen that your regular review with a higher-up falls during a Mercury retrograde, but if not, meeting with an authority figure to highlight past achievements can actually be in your best interest, given that Mercury's backspins promote reevaluation and communication about past events. Just make sure that you're presenting your case as clearly as possible. And even then, because miscommunication is more likely than usual, you'll want to be prepared to elucidate until your message has been thoroughly received.

Back up your files and be extra careful with tech. If you've heard this Mercury retrograde warning before, that's because it's solid advice. And yet sometimes, no matter how cautious you've been and how many backup hard drives you've used, crucial messages go rogue, the files required for that important project disappear into the ether, or your device glitches out to the point that it's unusable. That's when it can be helpful to reframe this experience as one that's testing but eventually going to strengthen your resilience.

Thriving in Love and Relationships

Whether you're single and swiping through potential matches, attached to a long-term love, or focused on nurturing your platonic bonds, the trickster planet's backspins can help you gain more clarity in your partnerships and friendships. That's because when wires get crossed, we're usually compelled to address not only the misunderstanding itself but ongoing dynamics. For example, perhaps you and your spouse have a frustrating miscommunication related to how you'll spend your anniversary, but the incident leads to a productive conversation about how you can more regularly build quality time into your busy schedules. During Mercury retrograde, we're nudged to do the kind of work that ultimately bolsters mutual understanding. Hold these pointers in mind to preempt exasperation and deepen your connections.

Pump the brakes when confusion takes hold. Any therapist will tell you that healthy communication is vital to a happy relationship. But even if you and your partner or best friend usually finish one another's sentences, Mercury backspins might make you feel like you're speaking different languages. Remind yourself that this is a possibility throughout the transit, and as soon as a conversation begins to go off the rails, slow down and get curious versus aggravated or defensive. By asking questions and doing your best to use "we" language (e.g., "Let's make sure we're on the same page" versus "Do you even know what I'm talking about?"), you'll be able to determine where the misunderstanding originated—and clear it up stat.

Weed out toxic bonds. A daunting but positive side effect of the reflection and self-work that Mercury retrogrades inspire: learning more about who you are, and in turn, with whom you want to surround yourself. Sometimes this shored-up self-awareness will serve as a catalyst for cutting ties with friends or lovers you've grown apart from or whose problematic behavior is now glaringly apparent. Recognizing the long-term benefits of walking away, like being genuinely happier and capable of standing even more strongly in your sense of self, can empower you to do so. You might initiate a conversation or write a thoughtful note that shares why you're stepping back. But in cases where the other person can't hear what you have to say and is prone to getting defensive, it may make sense to simply set and hold a boundary in the name of doing what's best for your well-being.

Know that encounters with people from your past are usually more about you than them. Should a former friend or ex-flame resurface, it might be for a productive or positive reason. Maybe a previous partner wants to collaborate professionally, or your college bestie, with whom you simply fell out of touch, now lives in your city, which leads to a happy revival of your friendship. But know that you're not necessarily meant to pick up where you left off with *everyone* who reenters your life. Since Mercury is the trickster planet, previous connections can pop up for no real reason other than to remind you of how far you've come. I theorize that, in some cases, the resurgence of a ghost from a past life is actually a test: They hold up a mirror for you to consider how much you've grown in the time that's passed since they were in your life. You have an opportunity to make a different choice than you did before based on who you are now. Self-reflection will help you realize whether certain past connections fit into your present-day life or if they offer nothing more than the IRL equivalent of reading an old diary.

Reassess shared goals. Whether you and your closest friend set out to train for a 5K together or you and your SO want to stick to a savings plan, you might want to (or actually need to!) have a check-in during Mercury retrograde. You can analyze your progress and any drawbacks of your current strategy and perhaps find that a few tweaks—or a full overhaul—can more effectively get you across the finish line.

Embrace time travel. Don't worry, you don't need a DeLorean. Even if you're not particularly sentimental, taking a walk down memory lane with a dear friend or partner can be a lovely bonding experience. For instance, though literal travel might require a little more planning and patience, Mercury retrograde is the perfect occasion for revisiting a romantic vacation spot with your sweetheart or taking a road trip to reunite with old friends. Or you might re-create a particularly memorable date night or recipe you've always enjoyed making together, or peruse old journals, photo albums, or videos.

Thriving in Wellness

The stereotypical issues that arise when Mercury is retrograde *can* be stressful, which obviously doesn't do wonders for your physical, mental, and emotional health. But you can manage that stress by embracing one of the must-dos of the transit: slow down. In the same way that we may think we need to have a lead foot to get ahead in our careers, we may believe we should be constantly working out, meal prepping, seeing specialists, or reading up on the latest wellness trends to feel our best. But when Mercury is moving backward, doing less is so much more—and it boosts both your inner peace and physical well-being during and following the transit.

Examine and edit existing aspirations. There are moments throughout the year and your life when you feel compelled to set a super-ambitious wellness goal. When Mercury's retrograde, gathering the information necessary to get that game plan off the ground can be truly frustrating. But this isn't to say it's *impossible*! Astrological events with conflicting messages happen simultaneously all the time. For instance, new moons happen roughly once—sometimes twice—a month, kicking off a brand-new lunar cycle that you can use for manifestation work. So smack in the middle of a Mercury retrograde there could be a gorgeous new moon that's conducive to setting a powerful intention related to fitness. But in general, instead of pursuing new goals, you can make the most of Mercury's backspin by getting crystal clear on what you want to achieve. You may be able to reimagine your endgame in a way that sets you up for even more success.

Review your mental self-care. Whether work stress has led to sleepless nights or a happy new chapter in your love life has you feeling revitalized, you know all too well just how much your mental and emotional well-being affect your physical health. More and more, we're talking about and connecting the dots between the mind and body. Mercury retrogrades are opportunities to get curious about how you're nurturing that connection. How are you tending to your mental health? How might you improve upon that approach? And how might that support your well-being overall?

Focus on short- and long-term stress relief. Being stressed out is often the impetus to overhaul your health priorities. The transit's push to go inward can help you become even more aware of your stressors and how you might be able to better manage them moving forward. You might find you're inspired to pick back up a practice you previously leaned on for stress relief, like attending a stretch class or seeing your favorite acupuncturist. But any restful and restorative activity, like getting a massage or spending time in nature, can be especially nourishing.

Tackle overdue health-related business. From a doctor's appointment you've been kicking down the road to a baffling explanation of benefits you've been meaning to make a phone call about, Mercury's retrogrades were made for tying up loose ends related to health and wellness. Still, you may very well encounter Mercury-fueled confusion and delays along the way. By expecting them, you'll be better prepared to deal with them head-on.

Set boundaries. The bright side of Mercury retrograde's frenetic, nerve-fraying tone? You can better understand your limits. Whether people in your life are asking more from you than you can reasonably give or you struggle with saying no, the messenger planet's backspin can be an opportunity to assert your needs and rethink your commitments in order to protect and strengthen your well-being.

Three Shortcuts to Feeling Empowered During Mercury Retrograde

1 CHECK YOUR MERCURY RETROGRADE HOROSCOPE. Whether you're interested in diving into self-study with a trusty astrology app or software (see page 164 for more) or want to work with a professional astrologer, you'll always do well to figure out how any given Mercury retrograde is interacting with your birth chart—check out page 88 for how to do this. Perhaps it's moving backward through your fifth house of romance and self-expression, which could mean you get a flirtatious text from someone you went out with years ago or you'll be compelled to go back to the drawing board on an artistic endeavor. Or maybe it's retrograde in your tenth house of career, so you'll be reflecting on your definition of long-term success, earning recognition for your work on a past project, or reconsidering a leadership role you previously turned down.

2 CONSIDER YOUR BIG SIX. You might also see if any or several of your big six (that's your sun, moon, Mercury, Venus, Mars, and rising signs) placements are in Gemini and/or Virgo. If so, you have a strong Mercury-ruled influence in your chart, which means you're likely to feel the planet's retrogrades more acutely than others. You also probably rely even more heavily on communication and tech than most people because, thanks to your natal Gemini and/or Virgo, you can't help but perpetually seek connection and information in both your personal and professional lives. Being so affected by these phases can serve as something of a crash course on how to best navigate them. Luckily, Gemini and Virgo placements translate to research savviness and supersharp communication skills, which you can lean on whenever retrograde wreaks havoc.

3 FIND OUT IF YOUR NATAL MERCURY HAPPENS TO BE RETROGRADE. If you were born when Mercury was retrograde, it's baked into your natal chart (for more on this, see page 93). While this can cause some self-doubt around how you come up with and share your ideas, it also means that when Mercury is moving backward, the world is encouraged to process information and communicate in a way that's more in line with how *you* think and express yourself. So you could be exceptionally productive, inspired, or capable of getting into a "flow" with Mercury-fueled endeavors—writing, having intellectually stimulating conversations, brainstorming, etc.—during these periods.

PART TWO

Making the Most of Mercury's Trip Through the Signs

As the sun travels across the ecliptic, we welcome a dozen distinctive seasons. Each of these twelve sun sign seasons affects us in its own way based on the unique characteristics of each sign. For instance, while the sun moves through proud, fixed fire sign Leo every year from July 22 or 23 through August 22 or 23, we're all more inclined to assert ourselves, step into the spotlight, and prioritize playfulness and pleasure. And when the sun is in dreamy, mutable water sign Pisces from February 18 or 19 through March 20, our imaginations and empathy soar.

Similarly, as Mercury moves either direct or retrograde through one of the twelve signs, it sets the tone for how we are currently inclined to express and absorb information, move through the world, and interact with technology. That said, by tracking its transits, you can more confidently and effectively connect with others. A couple ways to figure out the sign through which Mercury is currently transiting:

☀ Get an astrological planner or calendar (see page 163).

☀ Search online for a planetary ephemeris, which provides monthlong tables that track the transits of every planet. To interpret the ephemeris, be sure to look for the Mercury symbol (☿) and familiarize yourself with the symbols for each of the twelve zodiac signs (see the chart on page 16; you'll also find them in the following pages).

Aries

Mercury in Aries usually occurs in March/April.

When it's direct: The cardinal fire sign Aries is ruled by Mars, the planet of action, and in turn, Ram energy is dynamic, to-the-point, speedy, and often impatient. While Mercury is zipping ahead in this fast-paced sign, we're all inclined toward more direct communication that will ideally save everyone time. The first sign of the zodiac is also innately competitive and hyperfocused on coming out on top, even when "winning" versus "losing" isn't relevant to the matter at hand. For instance, when they're on the road, an Aries may strive to "beat" the GPS estimated time of arrival. That said, everyday conversations can get either playfully or seriously aggressive when the Ram's desire to one-up takes hold.

Tips for Mercury direct in ♈

* As one of the visionary cardinal signs, Aries loves new beginnings and coming up with and diving into big, bold game plans, so you can use Mercury's trip through the sign of the Ram to pitch trailblazing, original ideas.

* Aries wishes that everything was said—and ideally, *done*—yesterday. So this isn't the time to get lost in the weeds, ruminating on minor details and dragging out meetings or brainstorming sessions. Sticking to concise, key bullet points helps you reach your endgame much faster.

* With the planet of transportation in this fiery sign, your fellow drivers or commuters may be more hotheaded, impatient, and impulsive than usual. You always want to drive—or travel—defensively, but Mercury in Aries is a case to be even more self-protective.

When it's retrograde: The combination of the Ram's need to communicate at lightning speed paired with Mercury's slowdown can make for silly little errors that stem from failing to double-check crucial information. It might also lead to misunderstandings that have a higher chance of blowing up into fiery conflicts. And the impetuous nature of the cardinal fire sign could lead to making rash decisions on which you'll need to backtrack later.

Tricks for Mercury retrograde in ♈

* When Mercury's retrograde in Aries, slowing down could be even more challenging than usual, since the Ram is known to be a real speed demon. After all, it is ruled by Mars, the planet of action. Resist the urge to move hastily through important paperwork, interactions, or travel.

* Reflect on your own competitive nature—how is your desire to win, achieve, or one-up others serving you and how is it holding you back? And if you're anything but competitive, how might you be able to use Aries's fiery nature to amplify your drive in a way that supports your aspirations?

* If you have an ongoing disagreement with a friend, colleague, or loved one, this can be a fantastic time to get back in the ring and assert yourself again. Because Mercury retrograde supports introspection, you'll have a better sense of why you're taking a particular position, and you may be able to articulate it more clearly.

Taurus

Mercury in Taurus usually occurs in April/May.

When it's direct: The fixed earth sign Taurus is ruled by Venus, the planet of relationships and beauty, which makes Bull energy harmony-seeking, luxury- and pleasure-loving, and unhurried. When Mercury is in this deliberate sign, we're all likely to spend more time thinking and expressing ourselves. When we're pushed to come up with ideas, initiate a conversation, or step out of our comfort zones (think having to hone new skills on the job), we could respond by digging our heels in and moving at an even slower pace. Taurus is, after all, one of the fixed signs, which can make the Bull as resolute as it is obstinate. While Taurean determination comes in handy with following through, action plans that are totally out-of-the-box might be sidelined for more traditional or tried-and-true strategies now.

Tips for Mercury direct in ♉

* Because Taurus is associated with the Second House of Income, Mercury's time in the sign of the Bull is conducive to networking and research in order to step up your moneymaking efforts. Values are also Second House terrain, so use this time to find work and investment opportunities that align with your principles.

* Taurean-style communication is pragmatic thanks to its earth influence and diplomatic because it's ruled by Venus. Whether you're giving a presentation, making a pitch, or having a high-stakes conversation with a significant other, loved one, or friend, you'll be more capable of articulating yourself in a way that's grounded and gentle but direct.

* Because Taurus is so sensual and prefers experiences that utilize all five senses, make a conscious effort to explore and connect with the world in new ways through sight, smell, taste, touch, and sound. This could mean listening to different types of music or ASMR, exploring aromatherapy, doing a visual guided meditation, cooking with a spice or herb you've never tried before, or scrolling through photos of your favorite scenic spot.

When it's retrograde: The languorous nature of Taurus lends itself to the energy of Mercury's slowdown while also encouraging us to be more down-to-earth in the face of delays and setbacks. You can use this period to reexamine what's working and what's not in terms of personal finances. It's also favorable for double-checking bank account details (for instance, ensuring you weren't mistakenly overcharged for a purchase), reworking your budget and investment portfolio, and smoothing over tension with the person who signs your paycheck.

Tricks for Mercury retrograde in

* Self-worth is a subject that Taurus often grapples with as it's terrain covered by the Second House. Examine your beliefs, values, thought patterns, and wellness habits, and make tweaks where necessary in an effort to bolster your self-worth.

* Because Taurus rules material possessions, reflect on your spending and saving, particularly in terms of material objects. You could reform problematic shopping habits, learn more about sustainable gifting, or donate items you don't need anymore.

* Taurean thinking can be so all-or-nothing that during this transit, you may be more inclined to stubbornly adhere to a particular plan, even when the frenetic nature of Mercury retrograde is making it near impossible. While it might not come as naturally now, striving to be more adaptable can be a saving grace.

MERCURY'S JOURNEY THROUGH

Gemini

Mercury in Gemini usually occurs in May/June.

When it's direct: The mutable air sign Gemini is ruled by Mercury itself, meaning the planet is in domicile (in a sign that it rules) and therefore capable of firing on all cylinders when it passes through the sign of the Twins. As a social air sign informed by the messenger planet, Gemini's energy is curious, changeable, and clever. During this time, our perspective and communication tend to be more inquisitive, adaptable, and occasionally flighty. Gemini lives for gathering and disseminating information, so this is a wonderful opportunity for observation, conversation, research, travel, and utilizing technology. But the Twins tend to struggle with indecisiveness and are easily distracted and scattered, so you might collect a variety of ideas but not necessarily be driven to act on any of them—or you might feel compelled to bounce from one intriguing path to the next.

Tips for Mercury direct in ♊

✳ You may be looking for a new job or place to live, dating, or contemplating how to tackle an important project. Regardless of your focus, do your best to adopt a lighthearted and curious perspective. You'll likely pick up a bevy of details and spotlight a multitude of options, some that are useful and others that are red herrings. Giving yourself plenty of space to explore can be more productive than pushing for the answer.

✳ Gemini's animated, distractable communication style can be overwhelming, especially to anyone who's a big fan of predictability and order. Remembering that not every idea or proposal that comes your way is worth your attention can help you prioritize, stay on track, and avoid running yourself ragged.

✳ We're all more chatty when Mercury moves through Gemini, so there is often no better time to schedule a brainstorm, engage in flirty banter with a partner, or play a word game with friends. But Twins energy is about listening as much as it is about communicating, so it can be helpful to hold that in mind in social situations. Be prepared to hold boundaries—and have boundaries set on you—if, instead of having a real conversation, someone is talking for the sake of talking.

When it's retrograde: Mercury fuels Gemini's high mental energy and *go-go-go* nature, so its retrogrades through the sign of the Twins can feel especially frenetic, confusing, and glitchy. The desire to flit from one thing to the next, to express ourselves, and to absorb what others are sharing is frustrated, which can spur exasperation. Channel that spirited vibe into catching up with longtime connections. And apply Gemini's characteristic curiosity to reviewing information and relearning skills, which can leave you feeling even more on the ball once Mercury's direct.

Tricks for Mercury retrograde in ♊

* Because Gemini is associated with the Third House of Communication, you can more readily tend to old business with siblings and neighbors now. But wires may get crossed, so go slow, strive for diplomacy, and avoid new undertakings if possible.

* The Third House also involves short-distance travel, so re-create a previous weekend getaway or make plans that require a brief car or train trip.

(Just plan ahead for Mercury retrograde's signature slowdowns and delays.)

* Think back to a fulfilling learning experience, like taking an art class or working with crystals. You might hit the books once again. Or consider rereading favorite novels, watching beloved films, or going back to a museum you've always cherished— you might find you have an exciting new perspective.

Cancer

Mercury in Cancer usually occurs in June/July.

When it's direct: The cardinal water sign Cancer is ruled by the emotional compass of astrology—the moon—leading the Crab to be intuitive, nurturing, and compassionate. As Mercury travels through this sentimental sign, we're more inclined to speak from the heart and prefer interactions that allow for meaningful bonding as opposed to shallow communication. Family, security, and the creature comforts of home life are all top of mind for Cancer, so these themes will likely take precedence in our thoughts and interactions. Given the emotional lens through which the Crab sees the world, it might be tougher to tap into facts, rationality, and impartiality right now.

Tips for Mercury direct in ♋

✳ Thanks to Cancer's warm and fuzzy nature, the mood is right for sharing how you feel and squeezing in quality time with loved ones. And because Cancer is associated with the Fourth House of Home Life, you'll find it fruitful to bond over domestic activities like baking a family recipe or tending your garden.

✳ Cancers are ingratiatingly hilarious and even a little silly—traits that are more accessible to us all while Mercury is in the sign of the Crab. Seeking out opportunities to laugh can strengthen your connections with others.

✳ When pushed for more information than they're ready to share or brooding about something from the past, Cancer's signature crabbiness kicks in and they might shut down entirely until they've worked through whatever's coming up for them emotionally. You'll notice that everyone is more likely to exhibit this behavior when Mercury is in the cardinal water sign. Whether it's you or someone you're interacting with, embracing a Crab-like retreat to process emotions can ultimately help open lines of communication.

When it's retrograde: Mercury spinning back through Cancer sets the stage for reflecting on what's in your heart *and* what's on your mind. This period also lends itself to storytelling with relatives and revisiting traditions, although watch out for conflict stemming from misunderstandings with family members more than anyone else. And thanks to the Crab's affinity for home life, you can—and may have to—deal with renovations, redecoration, or repairs. Cancer's realm of the Fourth House also covers financial security, so it might be time to take a microscope to investments and savings accounts.

Tricks for Mercury retrograde in ♋

* Mercury retrograde in Cancer asks us to tend to our familial connections, so reconnect with loved ones you've been missing. If there was a time in the past when you didn't see eye to eye and you're still struggling with that conflict, you might attempt to smooth it over now.

* Given Cancer's association with the Fourth House, use this period to research and revise any plans related to real estate. Get your ducks in a row ahead of making a big move like signing a new lease, listing your home for sale, or diving into a renovation project.

* As information-gathering Mercury functions with less strength in a deeply emotional sign, you can anticipate moodiness that leads to miscommunications and vice versa. Hold space for emotions while striving to bring more objectivity into your interactions.

MERCURY'S JOURNEY THROUGH

Leo

Mercury in Leo usually occurs in July/August.

When it's direct: Leo is ruled by the sun, which bestows confidence on the fixed fire sign. And as a result of being guided by the brilliant, flaming star that serves as the center of the entire solar system, the Lion is bursting with optimism, drive, and a love of fun, romance, and sharing what's in its heart. As Mercury moves through this charismatic sign, we'll be drawn to stepping into the spotlight and feel more assured when asserting our desires. We're more prone to exaggerating and striving to be entertaining. This transit makes it possible to explore—and own—your sense of self. Creativity and self-expression are also the Lion's terrain, so you can open up more readily about your emotions, potentially in a playful way. Because Leo excels in leadership roles, it might be tougher to collaborate, be a team player, and hear others out.

Tips for Mercury direct in ♌

* Leo loves the roar of applause and soaking up positive attention, so now's your chance to open yourself up to whatever form of recognition you'd most appreciate. You might point out to a higher-up that you deserve credit for extra work you did on a project, investigate ways you can showcase an artistic hobby, or plan a luxurious vacation for your sweetheart.

* Communication is more passionate, confident, and direct while Mercury passes through the sign of the Lion. Avoid beating around the bush, hesitating, and apologizing when you have nothing to say you're sorry for. Now you have even more fuel to trust yourself, say exactly what you mean, and get right to the point.

* The fixed fire sign cares deeply about fostering identity and self-love and seeing others for who they are, which makes this a valuable time for celebrating what makes you shine and showering others with plenty of compliments on the same. You might be inspired to tell your best friend that you admire their parenting style and hope to emulate it when you have a child, or write your significant other a note detailing how you see they're working hard on a project close to their heart and you've got their back.

When it's retrograde: While Mercury moves backward through Leo, miscommunication could stem from a tendency to overstate the truth or see a situation from an overly optimistic, go-getter perspective. It's a wonderful opportunity to do intense inner work around identity, self-esteem, and building confidence. And given the Lion's connection to self-expression and pleasure, you might also be inspired to revisit an artistic outlet you enjoyed years ago or to reconnect with your most entertaining, fun-loving friends.

Tricks for Mercury retrograde in ♌

* Mercury's backspin in Leo can support self-reflection around leadership opportunities, perhaps on the job or in your personal life. Even if you have zero interest in managing others, use this period to tap into your inner boss.

* Because Leo is associated with the Fifth House of Self-Expression, this transit lends itself to recalling simple life pleasures and activities that you loved as a kid and revisiting them, perhaps with your own family, significant other, or a dear friend.

* As one of the fixed signs, Leo can be hardheaded and believe that their perspective is the only one worth listening to. That challenging trait could be magnified for us all while Mercury is retrograde in the sign of the Lion, sparking friction. The fix: striving to listen to and hold space for a variety of voices to weigh in.

Virgo

Mercury in Virgo usually occurs in August/September.

When it's direct: The mutable earth sign Virgo is ruled by Mercury itself, which means the planet is in domicile when it passes through the sign of the Maiden. Virgo's energy is cerebral, detail-focused, and analytical. When Mercury is in this pragmatic sign, we'll be more grounded and interested in being of service to others, particularly by gathering valuable information. This transit encourages you to be meticulous and organized so you can successfully complete any endeavor you've taken on. And heads up: You may find yourself in a frame of mind that's slightly more worrisome and pedantic than usual.

Tips for Mercury direct in ♍

☀ You can be incredibly precise when Mercury moves through Virgo. This is a wonderful moment to put your nose to the grindstone on projects you've been putting off because you need time to really dive in, like editing a proposal, creating a budget, or having a chat with your partner about how you can better share the mental load. Avoid nitpicking or allowing perfectionism to hold you back from experimentation.

☀ Get on top of your routine. If you want to foster better work-life balance or explore a new wellness plan, this is a period in which you can trade notes with friends and study up on potential ways to do that, given

Virgo's association with the Sixth House of Daily Routine and Wellness and affinity for self-improvement. All that information gathering can lay the groundwork for a concrete strategy. From start to finish, this process is one of the Maiden's greatest thrills in life.

☀ The nature of Mercury in Virgo allows us to examine the details that we lose sight of when looking at the big picture—or that we never even considered in the first place. Be sure you have a long-term vision in mind before spending time on minutiae, and continually make sure that whatever you're zeroing in on is in service of that greater purpose.

When it's retrograde: While Mercury is backing up through one of the two signs it rules, expect confusion around aspects of your day-to-day life that might seem small but are actually significant. After all, if you keep entering your password with one character off, you're going to get locked out. Wellness and routine are Virgoan territory, so we're nudged to slow down and reassess our approach to these areas of life.

Tricks for Mercury retrograde in ♍

✳ Because Virgo is associated with the Sixth House, you can use this time to resume a regular fitness regimen that fell by the wayside. You might also review a recently completed project with a more meticulous eye, or reflect on your current schedule and whether or not it's truly serving your goals in the long run.

✳ Virgo's knack for keying into specifics can come in handy now. Aim to be extra eagle-eyed while reading important documents, ask lots of questions, and spend time pulling together facts and figures, so you can more easily preempt misunderstanding.

✳ Virgoan energy is highly industrious, but it's possible to take that mentality too far and end up stressed out. Consider the practical habits that will support your inner peace, whether that's enjoying lunchtime walks or taking steps to protect your work-life balance. Give yourself grace to build momentum, as it could take until Mercury is direct to adopt any wholly new practice.

Libra

Mercury in Libra usually occurs in September/October.

When it's direct: Ruled by Venus, the cardinal air sign Libra is serenity-loving, social, and justice-seeking. Mercury's time in the sign of the Scales causes us to be more diplomatic, invested in prioritizing balance in our interactions and experiences, and interested in art and beauty. You can foster partnerships, mediate conflicts, and tackle aesthetic projects with the power of Mercury in this visionary sign. However, because Libra abhors conflict above all else, it might be tougher than usual to express anger, frustration, or any stereotypically "negative" emotion for fear of rocking the boat. In turn, you could be tempted to default to passive-aggressive behavior.

Tips for Mercury direct in ♎

* Because this time strengthens everyone's ability to make and keep the peace, reach out to someone with whom you've struggled to see eye to eye—you could find that you're able to boost and maintain mutual understanding.

* Symbolized by the Scales, Libra is naturally inclined to champion equity and tip the balance toward justice. You can more readily learn about and trade notes with others on charitable causes that you might invest time, energy, or money into.

* One-on-one conversations, ideation, and relating are all optimized now, given that Libra is associated with the Seventh House of Partnership. So if you want to increase efficiency on a project at work, be held accountable for sticking to a wellness routine, or feel more connected socially, pair up with a friend, loved one, or significant other.

When it's retrograde: While Mercury moves backward through Libra, relationship issues from the past that were left unsettled might require your attention. Misunderstandings could stem from you or others bending over backward to ensure that a situation is fair or free of conflict. You can meditate on how you want to show up in your partnerships and how you expect others to show up, which might lead to useful takeaways on reciprocity. This transit is also a chance to take stock of how balanced you're feeling emotionally and mentally.

LIBRA

Tricks for Mercury retrograde in ♎

* Because Libra is devoted to bringing more artistic value into the world, this is a lovely moment to express yourself in a visual way. You might be inspired to draw in a sketchbook or bake a gorgeous dessert. You might also give away accessories or jewelry you don't wear anymore and refresh your wardrobe (maybe with a cute look from a thrift store, which would be *really* Mercury retrograde in Libra), repaint your bedroom, or refurbish an antique store find.

* Do a progress report and reassess your approach to hitting a shared goal with a trusted companion. And if you're cohabiting or running a business with a partner, it's an especially fruitful time to revisit ongoing conversations related to sharing the workload.

* In an effort to sidestep conflict, Libran-style communication can lead to ambiguous statements, glossed-over issues, and sugarcoated information. All this could cause even more confusion, so it's best to be as direct as possible now. You can still lean on diplomacy, but not at the expense of clarity.

Scorpio

Mercury in Scorpio usually occurs in October/November.

When it's direct: The fixed water sign Scorpio is co-ruled by Mars, the planet of action and energy, and Pluto, the planet of transformation and power. This dynamic duo gives the Scorpion its laser-focused, magnetic, and intense vibe. Mercury's time in Scorpio causes us to be more emotional, private, passionate, and zeroed in on building intimacy. With the communication planet in a sign that's dynamic *and* deeply investigative, you're less likely to stand for superficial conversation. You can more readily dig beneath the surface to find out what's really going on, especially in relationships, as the water sign is associated with the Eighth House of Intimacy. This transit can simultaneously make it tougher to see nuance and engage in flexible thinking, given Scorpio's willful nature.

Tips for Mercury direct in ♏

* As Mercury moves through Scorpio, everyone is more apt to keep their cards close to the chest. While you might wish that a lover, friend, or family member would be more willing to open up and share what's on their mind, nudging could result in *more* radio silence. Instead, make it clear that you're ready to talk whenever the time is right. You may be surprised by how much more effective that approach is.

* Given the sign's association with the Eighth House, you can more readily explore and discuss your steamiest fantasies. You'll also do well to ask the tough questions that you're not always the most comfortable posing. An amplified willingness to examine and accept your fears and the aspects of life that are challenging to acknowledge and discuss (like anger, jealousy, possessiveness) can lead to enhanced self-awareness and relationships.

* Given the private, cryptic nature of Scorpio, you may find yourself in the same headspace as a guest at a murder mystery dinner party, assuming that everything is a clue, secret, or puzzle to be solved. Sure, that may be the case at times, but veer too far in this direction and you run the risk of paranoia.

When it's retrograde: You might face challenging communication around your closest bonds and joint resources, both of which fall under the Eighth House. Because Scorpio tends to be so obstinate, we're all more likely to refuse to admit we made a mistake and therefore need to revise our work, which can make for a lack of forward movement. This transit could lead to the exposure of secrets that you (or someone near and dear to you) have been attempting to keep. This isn't to say that these three weeks will be replete with interpersonal drama, but emotions may be heightened, which could eventually lead to a healing resolution.

Tricks for Mercury retrograde in ♏

* Whether you've been wanting to reach out to someone with whom you previously shared a close, meaningful connection or work on healing deep-rooted wounds inflicted by an intimate relationship, this transit is conducive to doing the emotional work of facing your past head-on.

* It's wise to use this period to review financial projects and investments, particularly wills, estates, and inheritances. You might be able to drudge up information on money that was previously hidden, misunderstood, or lost. On the flip side, it's best to wait to deal with unestablished asset-related endeavors, such as moving the ball forward on a new mortgage.

* Scorpios tend to be intensely family-oriented and innately respectful of spiritual traditions. You might be compelled to learn more about your ancestors (think creating a family tree) or interview senior relatives.

Sagittarius

Mercury in Sagittarius usually occurs in November/December.

When it's direct: The mutable fire sign Sagittarius is ruled by Jupiter, the planet of abundance and expansion, which also happens to be the largest planet in the solar system. So, it's no wonder that Sag drums up go-big-or-go-home, jovial, and knowledge-seeking energy. While the information-gathering planet moves through the sign of the Archer, communication could be fierier, more buoyant, philosophical, and unfiltered. This is a festive time when everyone's a little more gregarious, entertaining, and interested in being entertained. You could be more enthusiastic and eager to learn and to explore the world well beyond your comfort zone. Thanks to the inflating effect of Jupiter, this transit could also lead to hyperbole and extreme thinking.

Tips for Mercury direct in ↗

* Because straightforward Sagittarius prioritizes honesty and truth above all else, this is a fruitful time for having direct, to-the-point conversations. Jupiter's influence can infuse these talks with positivity and optimism.

* Sag is prone to proselytizing, so you or others in your sphere might end up getting on a soapbox more than usual during this transit. In these instances, it can be helpful to remember—and if necessary, point out—that opinions aren't facts.

* Mercury's time in Sag was made for dreaming *and* doing. The Archer is full of wanderlust and aims to live in—and make the most of—the moment. Taking a spontaneous, long-distance trip, learning a different language, or applying to a continuing education course would be supremely fitting and productive uses of this period.

When it's retrograde: This fire sign's penchant for extreme thoughts and self-expression could backfire. For instance, a compliment delivered in an over-the-top way might be mistaken as sardonic. And because Mercury is retrograde in the sign ruled by Jupiter, which has a magnifying effect on everything it encounters, the usual confusing, chaotic effects of the transit may be even more intense and apparent. Nonetheless, given Sagittarius's commitment to telling it as it is, you might be able to clear up misunderstandings rather quickly. And because Sag loves soaking up knowledge, this is a retrograde during which you can reimmerse yourself in valuable learning experiences and meditate on emotionally fulfilling ways to broaden your horizons (think shopping for ingredients you've never tried before in order to cook up a unique recipe that a loved one told you they've been craving).

Tricks for Mercury retrograde in ✗

✳ Associated with the Ninth House of Adventure and Higher Learning, Sagittarius is eager to forge into uncharted territory for the sake of having eye-opening experiences. While a Mercury retrograde through Sag might not be the ideal time to go globe-trotting, it is perfect for revisiting places or rereading books that can fulfill that desire to spread your wings. Rewatching old episodes of your favorite travel show or streaming a film in a different language could prove inspiring—and helpful once Mercury is direct.

✳ The Archer's signature shoot-from-the-hip style could fuel a foot-in-the-mouth moment—even more than usual. Whether you're the culprit or the target, dealing with the situation head-on could translate to better results than attempting to sweep it under the rug during this bluntly honest season.

✳ With the transit in high-spirited Sagittarius, it might be easier to laugh off typical Mercury retrograde moments, stay positive, and keep your eye trained on the big picture.

Capricorn

Mercury in Capricorn usually occurs in December/January.

When it's direct: The cardinal earth sign Capricorn is ruled by Saturn, the planet of commitment and boundaries. In turn, the Sea Goat is serious, diligent, and motivated. As Mercury moves through Cap, the way we connect with one another and think about the world around us becomes more pragmatic, concrete, and goal-oriented. This is the time of year when you can gain clarity around what exactly it will take to reach whichever summit you've had your eye on, and chances are, that'll be good, old-fashioned, satisfying work that you won't necessarily mind putting in extra hours in order to complete. Because Saturn oversees structure, this transit can support your ability to lay a solid foundation for long-term objectives.

Tips for Mercury direct in ♑

* You'll do well to initiate conversations with higher-ups and assert your own power. You can look for clarification and guidance or take on a leadership position. Information gathering charged by the grounded Sea Goat can support your most ambitious strides, in part because it's the sign associated with the Tenth House of Career.

* Capricorn energy encourages you to take initiative, especially when it comes to major aspirations. This transit could offer a fresh start.

* If you've been unsure of how to address an ongoing challenge, like the best way to pay down debt or take a romantic relationship to the next level, you'll find it easier than usual to land on practical, step-by-step solutions. And with Saturnian energy on your side, you can channel more perseverance.

When it's retrograde: This earth sign's laser focus on professional achievement can turn your attention to perfecting career matters. You might be compelled to do inner work around your definition of success, work ethic, and what you want to be recognized for. All the while, you'll need to preempt or smooth over miscommunication with authority figures. One significant silver lining of this transit: Cap is hardworking, practical, and innately comfortable with moving slowly and steadily toward a goal—all characteristics that lend themselves to making the most of this opportunity to look in the rearview before plowing ahead.

Tricks for Mercury retrograde in ♑

❋ Capricorn cares deeply about earning recognition for diligent industriousness. The Sea Goat sees the value in getting something right versus rushing. So, whether you're aiming for a new job offer or to be rewarded for work that you've already put in, reexamine and potentially revise your approach.

❋ No one likes butting heads (well, okay, except for maybe Aries!), and this transit could set up confusing interactions with people in a position of power—from bosses to health care providers— that set your teeth on edge. Reframe them as a chance to foster your own sense of authority, remembering that you have every right to ask as many questions as you want and to ensure your voice is heard.

❋ Your boundaries could be challenged now (for instance, your parents offer unsolicited advice about an upcoming event, like a holiday dinner or baby shower). Rethink how to best hold your ground. Even responding with different language than usual ("Thanks for sharing your opinion; it will be taken under consideration") could do the trick. And if you're on the flip side of this equation, you may find it beneficial to reflect on what drives you to push others' boundaries.

Aquarius

Mercury in Aquarius usually occurs in January/February.

When it's direct: Aquarius's modern ruler is Uranus, the planet of revolution, sudden change, and freedom. For that reason, any planet traveling through this air sign takes on a rebellious, idiosyncratic, and future-minded tone. As Mercury moves through the sign of the Water Bearer, we're more inclined to collaborate with others, get involved in humanitarian undertakings, shake up the status quo, invent, and innovate. Breezy and social, this energy is perfect for forging new friendships and nurturing existing platonic bonds. But Aquarius is one of the fixed signs, so we may also experience rigid, all-or-nothing thinking as well as debates and dustups that stem from one party digging their heels in as they opt to play the contrarian. After all, the Water Bearer is quite paradoxical in that the sign may struggle with obstinacy but also understands the value of being a team player.

Tips for Mercury direct in ♒

✳ Although it's important to give back no matter which sign Mercury is moving through, there's a special focus on it while the information-gathering planet is in altruistic Aquarius. You'll find you have extra wind in your sails to raise donations for a nonprofit that champions your values or get a petition going to create change in your community.

✳ The Aquarian perspective is as innovative and idealistic as it is willful. That said, this is a transit perfect for making progress on any forward-thinking venture. Just watch out for clinging so hard to your preferred end result that you refuse to be practical or hear others out.

✳ Whether you're trying to mediate a heated situation between family members or make the case for implementing an unconventional approach on the job, you'll find that Mercury in Aquarius sets the stage for rational, cooperative thinking and communication. But by the same token, it'll lend a cool, aloof vibe to interactions, so it may be best to calibrate expectations for passionate declarations.

When it's retrograde: Given the Water Bearer's association with the Eleventh House of Friendships, you can reunite with groups of friends (like your coworkers from your first big job). Because the fixed air sign is proudly rebellious, you can reflect on ways in which you'd like to stop adhering to particular conventions and strike out on your own (for instance, maybe it's time to figure out how you can bring more flexibility into your schedule in order to make a long-term dream a reality). With Mercury moving backward in a sign ruled by Uranus, which oversees electricity, this could be the transit during which you'll have no choice but to replace your car battery or rewire a whole room of your home. Take heart knowing that this is one retrograde during which we can all address irritating messes with breakthrough solutions.

Tricks for Mercury retrograde in ≋

* Join forces with community members to rethink the best approach to a group effort. By slowing down, you can step up your ability to be a team player.

* The Water Bearer can be contrarian, iconoclastic, and sarcastic, particularly when reacting to conventions or traditions. During this transit, some people might reflect on or question societal expectations. And when the communication planet isn't at full strength, this potentially antagonistic perspective might spur conflict. Lean on individuation, acknowledging that while a certain tradition or approach may not be for you or your friend/relative, it's cool to agree to disagree.

* This transit can support the resurrection of the most out-there, genius ideas, especially those related to Aquarian themes, such as science and community. Now's a fantastic time to flirt with revolutionary or rebellious game plans, which will be easiest to kick off once Mercury's direct.

Pisces

Mercury in Pisces usually occurs in February/March.

When it's direct: Neptune, the planet of illusion, dreams, and spirituality, rules the mutable water sign Pisces. As a result, the Fish is mystical, escapist, and artistic. When Mercury is in this perceptive sign, we're more empathic, intuitive, and capable of picking up on the subtext and feelings underlying what others are saying. This energy lends itself to having healing heart-to-hearts and channeling our most intense emotional experiences into creative or spiritually fulfilling outlets. At the same time, Neptune tends to cloud rational thought, so clear, concise, logical communication can be elusive now.

Tips for Mercury direct in ♓

* Tap into the beauty and power of the big-hearted Piscean perspective. You can more readily perceive others' needs and lend a shoulder to cry on. Keep in mind that you don't have to take on their challenges as your own in order to be there for your nearest and dearest.

* Pisces is highly flexible but also quite indecisive, open to whatever comes, whenever it comes. This hands-off approach supports imaginative, dreamy efforts like escaping into a novel or experimenting with a new creative outlet, but it's not the best for developing or executing a concrete, pragmatic plan that must be followed to a T.

* Given just how intuitive Pisces is, you'll do well to use this transit to connect with and honor your inner voice. We may all be a bit more people-pleasing during this transit, but if your gut says no, say no out loud.

When it's retrograde: You can get back to work on an artistic endeavor or dive back into emotionally fulfilling and even healing activities you previously put on pause. And because the mutable water sign is associated with the Twelfth House of Spirituality, expect this retrograde to be even sleepier than others. We're all encouraged now to make room in our hectic schedules to recharge and recover from Mercury's trip through the previous eleven signs. So it's possible you won't be as social as usual or you'll be just a bit more discerning about the people you're giving your energy to.

Tricks for Mercury retrograde in ♓

* Pick up where you left off with self-work on old wounds or emotional issues. This moment can be ideal for reviewing these topics with a therapist or mental health care provider.

* Slowing down is tough enough in our go-getter culture, but when the planet of communication is backtracking through Pisces, try to find more time for rest, daydreaming, and self-care—any of which can lead to a clearer, more refreshed perspective.

* Embrace Pisces's mutability and the fact that Mercury is not in tip-top shape, and do your best to give yourself a break when it comes to making hard-and-fast decisions. When you're pressured, a statement like "I need time to think about that" can come in handy and offer you a chance to check in with your heart— and to perhaps wait until Mercury is direct—before moving ahead.

Understanding Your Mercury Retrograde Horoscope

When you check out your natal chart (see page 12), you'll see that the cusp of each house is linked to a particular sign. Once you know the sign in which a Mercury retrograde is occurring, you can match that sign with the house in your own chart that the transit is lighting up (for example, if Mercury happens to be moving backward in Pisces, and Pisces is located on the cusp of your second house of income, the retrograde will involve themes related to that house, detailed below). By pinpointing the house that Mercury retrograde is affecting, you can make the most of the opportunities you'll be presented with over the three-week transit.

FIRST HOUSE OF SELF: Reflect on, revise, and reimagine your personal brand and how you want to show up in the world.

SECOND HOUSE OF INCOME: Rework your approaches to earning, saving, and budgeting while bolstering your self-worth.

THIRD HOUSE OF COMMUNICATION: Reconnect with old friends, nurture relationships with siblings if you have them, and cultivate patience when issues with technology and transportation arise.

FOURTH HOUSE OF HOME LIFE: Renovate or redecorate your nest while also nurturing your inner life, sense of security, and family.

FIFTH HOUSE OF ROMANCE AND SELF-EXPRESSION: Meditate on your creative process, how you want to share your voice, and how you can bring more playfulness, joy, and magic into your day-to-day.

SIXTH HOUSE OF WELLNESS: Check off health-related to-dos that have been left unfinished and reconsider how you're handling daily routines.

SEVENTH HOUSE OF PARTNERSHIP: Rethink how you're moving toward shared goals in your one-on-one bonds and reassess reciprocity.

EIGHTH HOUSE OF INTIMATE BONDS: Take a microscope to incomplete business related to joint resources and gauge your comfort level in your closest relationships.

NINTH HOUSE OF ADVENTURE AND HIGHER LEARNING: Tap into back-burnered desires to advance your skill set, broaden your horizons, or take a leap of faith.

TENTH HOUSE OF PUBLIC IMAGE AND CAREER: Muse about and potentially revise your professional endgame, resume an ongoing conversation with an authority figure, and tie up loose ends in your work life.

ELEVENTH HOUSE OF FRIENDSHIPS AND LONG-TERM ASPIRATIONS: Go back to the drawing board on a collaborative project, reconnect with aspirations you've lost sight of (perhaps by reading an old journal), and reassess your platonic bonds and the communities you're a part of.

TWELFTH HOUSE OF SPIRITUALITY: Slow down, pay more attention to your dreams, and prioritize rest, which is not only well-deserved in and of itself but can also result in more vitality down the road.

PART THREE

Owning Your Unique Mercury Magic

Just as your sun sign generally plays the leading role in any conversation about natal astrology, your ascendant (or rising sign) often gets all the credit for your outward personality. It's the sign you lead with, the one that colors how people perceive you at first blush. But once you begin interacting with others, your Mercury sign is quick to take over. If everyday life is a party, the ascendant is the outfit you're wearing as you make your entrance. But as soon as you greet the host, mingle with other guests, share who you are, and learn the rules of the hilarious game in which everyone's participating, your Mercury is running the show. Your natal Mercury placement is also at the helm during more introspective moments, like when you're preparing the best strategy for networking with a client you want to impress or working through racing thoughts by writing them down.

That said, knowing your Mercury sign can help you better understand not only how you articulate what's on your mind but also your thought processes, how you learn, and the ways in which you make decisions as well as gather, share, and assimilate information. Holding all that in mind will help you strengthen your self-awareness, express yourself more effectively, and improve your bonds—not to mention make for smoother sailing when transiting Mercury is up to its trickster ways, whether it's making a tense angle to another planet or going retrograde.

How to Find Your Mercury Sign

Thanks to its proximity to the sun, Mercury is usually in the sign that the sun is occupying, if not the sign before or after it. That said, you can safely assume that if your sun is in Aries, for example, your Mercury sign is either Aries, Pisces (which precedes Aries), or Taurus (which follows Aries). Still, the most accurate way to pinpoint your Mercury sign is to take a look at your birth chart (see page 12) and look for the Mercury symbol (☿). It will accompany the symbol of the zodiac sign that it was in when you were born as well as the degrees of that sign. Another quick way to pinpoint your Mercury sign: Visit my website, maressabrown.com, where you can use my Mercury sign calculator. You could also run an online search for "Mercury sign calculator."

What It Means If You Were Born During Mercury Retrograde

Because Mercury is retrograde so frequently—approximately nine to twelve weeks out of the year—it's fairly common to be born during the astrological event. In fact, this is the case for about 25 percent of people.

If you were born during a Mercury backspin, you have "natal Mercury retrograde," which is denoted on your chart with an "Rx" or lowercase "r" next to the Mercury glyph—or you'll see that the degrees of your Mercury placement are red as opposed to black. This means:

✷ You're more likely than others to take your time thinking about what you want to say and how to say it.

✷ You might express yourself in a way that others perceive as a bit quirky, offbeat, or just plain original.

✷ You're especially inventive, creative, and perceptive.

✷ You were born with a unique opportunity to learn even more about communication and the mind than others.

✷ You sometimes feel misunderstood and will need to put in a little more work than others to express yourself fully, authentically, and confidently. But this is a task you were born to take on.

Aries

You think and express yourself at a lightning pace. Getting right to the point is a virtue you applaud in others. Not only do you abhor sharing your thoughts in a fussy, long-winded manner, taking in information that is presented this way also feels exasperating to you. Being so direct as well as authoritative works in your favor when you step into leadership positions that you're well-suited for and drawn to. You're driven to be the first to present what you believe is a winning pitch in a meeting or to share what you've learned about a hot new topic. Because Aries is ruled by Mars, the planet that rules aggression and was named for the God of War, you can sometimes be verbally combative, prodding those you're interacting with to disagree or even fight with you because you find the prospect of "beating" them in a war of words thrilling and intellectually gratifying.

SUPERPOWERS

You're boldly assertive. When it comes to speaking your mind, you can be truly fearless. Whether there's an issue with a dish you ordered at a restaurant or you need to set a boundary with a loved one, you won't shy away from stating the facts plainly, which can be a wonderfully effective way to ensure you're heard.

You can be playful. Your sense of humor is silly and childlike, which others find endearing and fun.

You blaze trails. Because you value being the first to pick up on a growing trend, you're often the one who alerts your friends or colleagues of the next big thing.

CHALLENGES

Being overly direct can backfire. Aries is associated with the First House of Self for a reason. Because you're simply stating what's on your mind, it's not your instinct to consider how your words might affect someone else before you say them. (Though you might think about it *after* the fact.) In turn, your communication style may sometimes be perceived as insensitive.

You struggle to be thorough. Because you hate to dwell, you often skip over details, which could get you in trouble when you're expressing yourself in a situation that requires minutiae, like, say, a conversation about money or travel.

You can be fast to a fault. You can be impulsive, offering up or taking in information before thinking through potential consequences, such as making embarrassing mistakes or introducing errors. For instance, you might hastily shoot off a strongly worded email to the wrong recipient or text your friends inaccurate details about an upcoming event in an effort to be the first to deliver the news.

LIKE-MINDED MATCHES

People who have Mercury or other big six placements in confident Leo or straight-shooter Sagittarius (fellow fire signs) share your enthusiasm, energetic sense of adventure, and knack for delivering information in a way that's passionate and to the point. You and free-spirited Aquarius share a passion for independence and individualism, while curious Gemini is perhaps the one sign that can keep up with your excitable, swift pace.

TOUGHER CONNECTIONS

People born with Mercury or other big six placements in peace-loving Libra (your opposite) may bristle at your affinity for conflict and competition, while heartfelt, sentimental Cancers and slow, steady Capricorns will also struggle to get on the same fiery and furious page as you.

Taurus

Your communication style is grounded, steady, and composed. When presented with a proposal, new idea, or decision that needs to be made, you like to think it through, priding yourself on pragmatism over speed. In fact, you're quite deliberate when it comes to problem solving as well as expressing yourself. Rarely leaning on small talk, you prefer to exchange information that's practical, concrete, and of clear value to you. Thanks to social Venus, Taurus's ruling planet, you're able to tell it like it is in an endearing, likable way. A dry sense of humor and sarcasm are absolutely in your wheelhouse. And because Taurus is innately in tune with all five senses, it's important to you to take in the world around you through scent, touch, taste, sight, and sound.

SUPERPOWERS

You can easily focus and follow through. The fixed energy of the Bull makes it possible for you to zero in on what's most useful to you or others and basically block out everything else, which can optimize your productivity.

You have a long fuse. Although anger can spur sudden, stormy outbursts for many people, your ability to take your time landing on the best way to express yourself applies even when you're losing your cool. Being measured in this way can keep your interactions with others fairly even-keeled.

You're a natural at steering the ship. Your down-to-earth ways and affinity for sticking to the facts support any aspirations you might have to step into a managerial position. Even in your personal life, friends and loved ones feel like they can lean on you for trustworthy guidance and reality checks.

CHALLENGES

You can be hardheaded. Taurus is symbolized by the Bull, after all. Whether you've made up your mind about a work-related strategy, an approach to dating, or a long-term investment plan, you're apt to dig your heels in. Your preference for what's tried, true, and comfortable could keep you from finding new solutions or experiencing growth.

You can drag your feet so long that you miss out. Being sensible and cautious can be to your detriment if it inhibits you from having conversations, making decisions, or researching valuable information before the moment passes you by.

By being so pragmatic, you could skip a chance to be lighthearted. You want everything you learn and absorb to have a real-world application, which is admirable but can also come at the expense of losing out on experimentation, exploration, and fun.

LIKE-MINDED MATCHES

Leading with common sense is something you share with people born with Mercury or other big six placements in fellow earth signs: service-oriented Virgo and industrious Capricorn. You might also find harmony with an intuitive Cancer or Pisces.

TOUGHER CONNECTIONS

You may find yourself at an impasse with people who have their Mercury or other big six placements in deeply emotional, fixed Scorpio, your opposite sign, as they are intensely invested in their heart whereas you prefer to lean on rationality. And because Leo and Aquarius placements are also fixed, all-around obstinacy could lead to headbutting.

Gemini

Because you were born with the messenger planet in its domicile, you're nothing short of an uber-social supercommunicator who prefers to be perpetually on the go. Chatty, inquisitive, and thirsty for new info pretty much 24/7, you're happiest when interacting with others, reading the news, using social media—basically doing anything that allows you to connect and learn. It can be tough for you to stick with one hobby or maybe even get especially passionate about one subject over another because you'd prefer to scatter your lively mental energy across a wide variety of topics. You're not only quick-witted and a fan of wordplay but also capricious in how you express yourself. One minute you might be bubbly and characteristically loquacious, but in the next instant, you're quiet and aloof.

SUPERPOWERS

You soak up new information like a sponge. Working on a whole new skill set for your job? Getting to know a new neighbor? Either way, you're genuinely curious and generally open-minded, which can lead to professional and social opportunities galore.

You're wildly adaptable. While some people fear switching gears, you pretty much live for it. You can seamlessly step into a new position at work or morph from attached to single with about as much as a shrug.

You're clever and entertaining. Your innate approach to self-expression is spirited, lively, witty, and fun, which others are sure to pick up on and find humorous and amusing.

CHALLENGES

You favor logic over feelings. Gemini tends to be cerebral, preferring to come at problem solving and communication through a mental lens, which means it's not your first instinct to dive into complex, emotional conversations.

You find it challenging to tune in to your inner voice. Your mental energy can be so high that all those buzzy thoughts and your desire to constantly be on the go can cause you to be disconnected from both your intuition and your spiritual side.

You can be overly critical. Whether a friend is telling you about a potential partner or your colleague has asked for your opinion of their presentation, you're hyperaware of all the details, which can lead you to nitpick. And if your own anxiety is spiking, you're even more likely to exhibit this behavior.

LIKE-MINDED MATCHES

You'll notice that people born with Mercury or other big six placements in fellow air signs, diplomatic Libra and humanitarian Aquarius, are just as invested in socializing as you are. You also click well with wide-eyed, dynamic Aries and Leo placements who love being on the move just as much as you.

TOUGHER CONNECTIONS

You may be aggravated by people born with Mercury or other big six placements in adventurous, philosophical Sagittarius, which is your opposite, given that you're not as opinionated as they are. And deeply feeling Pisces might wish you'd give your heart as much say as your head once in a while. You might also find it hard to see eye to eye with traditionalist Capricorn, as they're a big fan of slow, steady, conservative strategizing versus your more playful, experimental, scattershot approach.

Cancer

You're sensitive, perceptive, heartfelt, and nurturing in your approach to communication. You're more at ease in the world of emotions than you are with hard-and-fast logic, which means you're apt to process and deliver information through the lens of the mood you're in. So, if you've had a stressful day at work, your crabbiness is no doubt going to bleed into that catch-up call with your best friend. And should you face a complex or frustrating situation, you'll retreat into your shell, going into "do not disturb" mode until you've figured out how you want to proceed. Cancer is ruled by the moon, astrology's emotional compass, which oversees how one cares for others and wants to be cared for, instincts, and security. This shows in your innately compassionate perspective as well as how you interact with your loved ones and express your thoughts in a way that's soothing and emotionally intelligent.

SUPERPOWERS

You can pick up on emotional subtext better than almost any other sign. For that reason, you make people feel truly heard—even if they're not saying everything that's on their mind.

You're naturally funny. You have an ingratiating, at times goofy sense of humor that you effortlessly weave into everyday conversation and life. You take a lot of pride in setting up the perfectly timed comedic moment or spot-on delivery of a sidesplitting punchline, and it means the world to you when your antics spur a laugh riot.

You're a pro at filing away and recalling memories. Because you're so sentimental, you have a knack for remembering and reminiscing about how various experiences in your life felt. You revel in paging through old photo albums, telling stories about collectibles you've held on to, or detailing a particularly magical first kiss.

CHALLENGES

You can be defensive. Your sensitivity may make you feel vulnerable to getting hurt by others. When you're afraid that an emotionally trying situation from your past is about to repeat itself, you have the tendency to either lash out or shut down and retreat into your shell before thoroughly assessing the present moment (which could be a case for diving into self-work that boosts your awareness around this tendency).

Your mood can color your self-expression to a fault. You're a big-picture thinker, but it can be tough to see the full scope when you're consumed by a particular feeling. Sometimes you have to step outside of yourself to get clear on the facts.

Your empathy might interfere with your sense of self. Caring for others comes naturally to you, but identifying too closely with someone else's emotions or opinions can cause you to lose sight of what is in your heart and on your mind.

LIKE-MINDED MATCHES

You can organically trade ideas with people born with Mercury or other big six placements in fellow water signs, intense Scorpio and dreamy Pisces, because they perceive the world and express themselves in an emotionally driven way like you. You'll also find harmony with a kindhearted, service-oriented Virgo and sensual, homebody Taurus.

TOUGHER CONNECTIONS

You may struggle to see eye to eye with someone born with Mercury or other big six placements in stoic, industrious Capricorn, your opposite sign, because you have such contrasting priorities. You also bristle at Aries's curt communication style and Libra's airy impassivity.

Leo

You're theatrical, sunny, individualistic, and self-assured when delivering and absorbing information. Because your Mercury sign is ruled by the sun, you have creative, grandiose ideas that you're fired up to share with just about anyone who will listen. You're exuberant and optimistic, skilled at convincing others to adopt whatever bold game plan you're advocating for. You also delight in being your friends' and colleagues' greatest cheerleader. You are a natural at running any show—whether that's standing in front of the boardroom, keeping your household in order, or literally directing a play—and you revel in the spotlight, earning applause for your contributions to any big-picture conversation. In fact, you're an adept storyteller who has the ability to enchant others by piecing together a narrative with dramatic, artistic flair. Aware and proud of your talents, you could be easily wounded—and apt to check out—when you feel like what you bring to the table isn't being fully heard or valued by others. In turn, you might opt to look for a more receptive audience.

SUPERPOWERS

Your confidence is contagious. You express yourself in a way that's so authoritative, charismatic, and self-possessed that it not only commands people's attention but also inspires them to be equally centered in themselves.

You're as fun-loving as you are captivating. You're the party guest who can effortlessly enthrall the crowd or the member of your friend group who can turn a regular weeknight hang into a memorable and entertaining time.

You're driven. You don't shy away from dreaming up and thinking through large-scale undertakings that others might deem too ambitious.

CHALLENGES

You might exaggerate or brag. Overconfidence—or insecurity that's masked by faux self-assuredness—could translate to boastfulness.

You might struggle to adapt. As a fixed sign, once you've made up your mind or landed on an agenda, you're not the biggest fan of having to pivot.

Being a team player can be difficult at times. In instances that call for contributing your thoughts alongside colleagues or friends, all who expect and are entitled to equal airtime, you might get aggravated because you'd rather be the one running the show.

LIKE-MINDED MATCHES

You'll hit it off with people whose Mercury or other big six placements fall in fellow fire signs, go-getter Aries and wanderlust-charged Sagittarius, because they're as enthusiastic, action-oriented, and passionate as you. You'll also sync with a beauty-loving Libra or social Gemini who appreciates your joie de vivre.

TOUGHER CONNECTIONS

People born with Mercury or other big six placements in community-focused, quirky, and future-minded Aquarius, your opposite sign, might frustrate you with their contrarian take and need to focus on what's best for the greater good versus the individual. Similarly, you might find it trying to connect with other fixed signs, hardheaded Taurus and intense, power-seeking Scorpio.

Virgo

You're service-oriented, analytical, thoughtful, sensitive, and perpetually striving to pinpoint and prioritize the most helpful information possible. Being that Virgo is ruled by Mercury itself—and the messenger planet is exalted (meaning able to function at its strongest) in the sign—your natal Mercury is especially powerful and results in you being a natural supercommunicator. You often make an impression on others with your quick wit and eagerness to learn. You're the person your friends lovingly refer to as "the human thesaurus" or the one they'll text for recommendations for everything from the best date night spot to the go-to acupuncturist in town. In fact, you endear yourself to others by always offering plenty of thoroughly researched advice and a shoulder to lean on. Because you're an innate information gatherer, your mind is often buzzing a mile a minute, which can lead to overthinking. But you'll usually figure out how to get back on track rather quickly as you're generally efficient, rational, and pragmatic in your problem solving and thinking.

SUPERPOWERS

You're a self-improvement pro. You're on a mission to be a better version of yourself—mentally, emotionally, physically—and are keen to gather all the details necessary to get there. No wonder friends and loved ones turn to you when they're motivated to bolster their well-being.

You're meticulous. You care deeply about making sure anything you're sharing with the world is accurate, which is sure to earn you recognition from appreciative colleagues, friends, and loved ones who know they can rely on you for valuable, properly cited, authoritative intel.

Behind your high mental energy is a deep sense of caring for others. While you may have a rep for being overly rational and at times a bit aloof, you're most motivated to apply your cognitive skills to helping your nearest and dearest. Nothing gives you more satisfaction than pinpointing must-see attractions to hit during a vacation with friends or finding the perfect recipe for a special, healthy dish your family will love.

CHALLENGES

You can contend with anxiety and self-criticism. Wired to overthink, your mind might drift to worrying about the future or get stuck on insecurities (which could end up being projected onto others). For that reason, you'll benefit from practicing mindfulness and self-compassion.

When others can't keep up with your quick mental energy, you may lose your cool. You think and communicate swiftly, which can create a disconnect with people who are operating at a different pace.

You're overly perfectionistic. You can be so type A at times that it hinders your ability to present your ideas. (As someone with Mercury in Virgo, I often self-motivate with the mantra "Done is better than perfect," a common phrase popularized by Virgo sun Sheryl Sandberg.)

LIKE-MINDED MATCHES

You'll click with people born with Mercury or other big six placements in fellow earth signs, deliberate Taurus and hardworking Capricorn, because they're pragmatic like you. You'll also harmonize with a thoughtful Cancer, who shares your nurturing communication style, or a deeply caring Scorpio.

TOUGHER CONNECTIONS

People born with Mercury or other big six placements in spiritually driven Pisces, your opposite sign, could be arduous to click with, given how fueled they are by feelings whereas you're generally focused on facts. And while you might appreciate how the other mutable signs, changeable Gemini and unfiltered Sagittarius, are as adaptable as you, their communication styles could feel out of sync with your own.

Libra

♎

You're social, beauty-loving, and diplomatic. Because the way you communicate is influenced by Venus, the planet of art, romance, and harmony, you come off as charming, likable, and a true people person. You light up more than usual when you're one-on-one, as Libra is associated with the Seventh House of Partnership. One of your most notable characteristics is the ability to communicate in a way that is sure to avoid ruffling any feathers. And if you have no choice but to deliver info that could potentially trigger a negative response, you'll go to painstaking lengths to preempt a conflict. Libra is symbolized by the Scales for a reason: You care deeply about balance and justice, so you can easily step into the role of mediator. At the same time, your need to ensure all sides are heard can inhibit you from taking a stand.

SUPERPOWERS

You know what's good. Because you're so open-minded and want to consider all possible flavors, opinions, voices, and destinations, you're able to enjoy a wide variety of experiences. In turn, it's easy for you to become a connoisseur—particularly when it comes to the finer, pleasurable (Venusian!) things in life, such as wine, art, and gourmet food.

You're the ultimate buddy. You're wired to sync your brain with a BFF, coworker, significant other, or loved one, and you excel at getting any shared goal—a workout, a deadline, a grueling move—across the finish line.

You're the ultimate diplomat. Whether you have to tell a friend that she has something in her teeth or deliver a less-than-stellar review to an employee, you're truly clever when it comes to presenting sensitive information in a gentle way.

CHALLENGES

You can be a people pleaser. Your desire to prevent others or yourself from having to contend with an uncomfortable interaction is commendable, but aiming to avoid any rockiness whatsoever is both unrealistic and stressful.

You might sacrifice your own feelings for fairness. In striving to ensure you're giving equal weight to all the voices around you, you could lose sight of your own emotions and end up resentful for it.

Because you'd rather avoid being aggressive at all costs, you end up being passive-aggressive. Keeping your true feelings at bay for too long can backfire.

LIKE-MINDED MATCHES

You thrive in relationships with people born with Mercury or other big six placements in fellow air signs: curious Gemini and personable Aquarius. You'll also get a kick out of a charismatic Leo who can go toe to toe with you when it comes to making a charming, sparkling impression on everyone they meet as well as a gregarious Sag.

TOUGHER CONNECTIONS

You'll be thrown by people born with Mercury or other big six placements in debate-loving, direct, competitive Aries, your opposite sign, because they express themselves in a completely dissimilar way. Meanwhile, you struggle with tenderhearted Cancers whose emotional focus feels foreign to your airiness and stoic Capricorns whose attachment to rules, tradition, and strict structure clashes with your point of view.

Scorpio

You're a magnetic, intuitive, and downright fearless communicator with a razor-sharp ability to zero in on the key point of any interaction. You're also keenly tuned in to emotional subtext. Because Scorpio is ruled by action-oriented Mars and transformative Pluto, you're passionate and adept at uncovering hidden truths and shedding light on taboo topics from which most people would shy away. You have the ability to assert disdain in a chilly, powerful way that can leave people reeling. The Scorpion is exceedingly private—and the most secretive sign—which means you have no interest in divulging how you feel or detailing your personal experience to just anyone. Even once you're prepared to voice your emotions, you're calculated about timing, and chances are you'll share in a direct, cool, and commanding way.

SUPERPOWERS

Your investigative skills are off the charts. Whether you're solving a puzzle on the job, helping a friend figure out why their ex ghosted, or deducing what will happen on the season finale of your favorite TV show, detective work comes naturally to you.

You're a passionate defender of loved ones. Your reverence for the people you care about—especially family and likely certain colleagues—is so intense that you usually champion and defend them without question.

Your love of intrigue inspires others to dig deeper. As a result of your tendency to question what might be happening behind closed doors or beneath the surface, you get other people thinking, too.

CHALLENGES

It's hard for you to rein in suspicion. Because you're so adept at shining a spotlight on ulterior motives and secrets (and you enjoy doing so), you might assume there's something nefarious going on when it's actually nothing at all.

You can be power-seeking to a fault. Not unlike Aries (also ruled by Mars), you're often strategizing and even falling down all-consuming rabbit holes to identify how you can come out on top.

You're easily fixated. Thanks to Scorpio's modern ruler, Pluto, which oversees obsession, you tend to get hooked on a specific agenda, perspective, philosophy, or hobby. While this can set you up to become an undisputed expert, it might also prevent you from exploring new terrain.

LIKE-MINDED MATCHES

You're on the same page as people born with Mercury or other big six placements in fellow water signs: sentimental, heartfelt Cancer and mystical, artistic Pisces. You also enjoy trading detailed notes with an astute, probing Virgo and striving for recognition alongside a similarly driven Capricorn.

TOUGHER CONNECTIONS

You might find you're aggravated by people whose Mercury or other big six placements are in your opposite sign, sensible Taurus, given their desire to prioritize pragmatism over emotional intensity. You're also prone to clash with similarly fixed Leos and Aquarians who share your willful mindset.

Sagittarius

You communicate in an upbeat, proactive, buoyant manner. After all, Sag is ruled by Jupiter, the planet of abundance, which also happens to oversee higher learning and philosophy. This expansive planet's influence means you're psyched to explore uncharted waters and absorb new knowledge. The bigger, bolder, and broader the concepts, the better, as minutiae tends to make your eyes glaze over. You'll then offer up what you've learned to others as a gift that will bolster their wisdom. Freedom of limitless expression is so important to you that you're prone to getting on a soapbox. You might also latch onto hyperbole, declaring an experience "absolutely amazing" or "The Worst Ever." You can be wonderfully cheerful, engaging, and even a bit over-the-top when championing others. And your predisposition for shooting from the hip and saying exactly what you think without running it through a diplomacy filter might catch people off guard—but also crack them up.

SUPERPOWERS

You're always pumped to get out of your comfort zone.
Long-distance travel and honing new skill sets (especially
learning different languages!) are your forte.

You're a natural entertainer. There's an innate showmanship to
your communication style that makes it easy for you to transfix a
crowd. You're a hilarious storyteller and enjoy expressing yourself
artistically, perhaps through comedy, music, or over-the-top
fashion, for example.

You care deeply about what's right and wrong. You have a strong
sense of justice, are quick to stand up for causes you believe in,
and will be the first to give a passionate, impromptu speech in
defense of what you see as righteous.

CHALLENGES

You might conflate opinions and facts. Knowing your own mind
and heart is truly a strength of yours. But at times, you'll argue
that a belief is a fact when that might only be the case to you.

Your unfiltered thoughts can sting. Because you value the truth
above all else, you'd rather say exactly what you think versus
sugarcoating it, but certain interactions with people in your circle
might call for a bit more sensitivity.

You're impatient. Whether you're catching up with a friend or meeting with clients, you want to get right to the heart of the matter ASAP. Surface-level chitchat, being required to follow a particular protocol or structure, or dancing around the subject at hand can cause you to lose your cool.

LIKE-MINDED MATCHES

You hit it off with people born with Mercury or other big six placements in fellow fire signs: loyal, dynamic Leo and go-getter, playful Aries. You'll also find that animated conversation ignites with free-spirited, future-minded Aquarius and fun-loving, friendly Libra.

TOUGHER CONNECTIONS

People whose Mercury or other big six placements are in inquisitive Gemini, your opposite sign, are as eager to learn as you but tend to be more lighthearted, less philosophical, and not as interested in forming an opinion, which may agitate you. You might also butt heads with fellow mutable signs, detail-driven Virgo and tenderhearted Pisces, whose sensitivities feel unfamiliar to you.

Capricorn

Y ou have a no-nonsense, methodical, steady approach to communication. Because the Sea Goat is ruled by Saturn, the planet of hard work, boundaries, and commitment, you prioritize structure and gravitate to information that is reputable, credible, and time-tested. For example, you're not one for saying yes to a new experience or learning opportunity if it's not practical, useful, and aligned with the goals you're working toward. Conversations in which friends or colleagues are gossiping or haphazardly flitting from one topic to the next irritate you because you're so systematic and logical. Small talk tends to get under your skin because it feels pointless and, for that reason, boring. Appearing authoritative is important to you; therefore, one of your greatest worries is appearing clueless, foolish, or inept when expressing yourself. Bear in mind that you harbor relentless pragmatism and industriousness, which translate to being exceptionally productive. Once you commit to tackling any kind of project, you'll surely cross the finish line.

SUPERPOWERS

You're a master fact-checker. Saturn's influence is a bit cynical, which serves you well when it comes to making sure you're getting the correct information, whether it's talking to your doctor or strategizing with coworkers.

You're methodical. Intent on creating logical systems and laying practical groundwork to get results, you think and communicate in a highly disciplined way. You may be shameless about taking your time to arrive at a decision, which could be irksome to people who want to push ahead at a snappier pace (but that's not your problem!).

You have a dry sense of humor. As hardworking and grounded as you are, you also get your social circle laughing by delivering gut-busting quips while maintaining a poker face.

CHALLENGES

You find it tough to divert from traditions. Because you're so concerned with following the rules, you could miss out on chances to experiment, be playful, or explore uncharted terrain.

You can be overly coolheaded. Due to your desire to be taken seriously, you sometimes present your thoughts in an exceedingly careful, stiff style that might inhibit you from fully connecting with people.

You might come off as harsh. As the taskmaster planet, Saturn is like the stern professor of the sky, so your communication style might come off that way at times. You applaud regulations and people who adhere to them, so should they end up off the beaten path, you might come down on them harder than necessary.

LIKE-MINDED MATCHES

Your communication style is compatible with people whose Mercury or other big six placements are in fellow earth signs: tenacious, sensual Taurus and logical, meticulous Virgo. You'll also see eye to eye with equally driven Scorpio and find that you and spiritual Pisces have much to learn from one another.

TOUGHER CONNECTIONS

You may be bewildered by people born with Mercury or other big six placements in nurturing, deeply feeling Cancer, your opposite sign, because it's hard for you to relate to their mood-fueled self-expression. And you're aggravated by impulsive Aries's lightning-fast approach to interactions and balance-craving Libra's reluctance to pick a side and stick to it.

Aquarius

Your communication style is rational, friendly, and unapologetically quirky. Because your modern ruler is Uranus, the planet of rebellion and sudden change, you take great pride in embracing the unconventional. You approach new information with a slight bit of cynicism, and in conversations with friends or colleagues, you play devil's advocate or opt to be an outright contrarian. Not only do you seek out intellectual debate for your own mental stimulation, you also have no interest in agreeing or conforming to other people's beliefs until you've thoroughly analyzed them to ensure they align with your unique perspective. Rarely will you adopt an idea or be okay with heading down a particular path because it's what's expected of you. Endlessly defensive of your individuality, you take great pride in offering up offbeat ideas or progressive proposals. You attract quite a few friends and acquaintances with your future-minded insights, free-spirited vibe, and humanitarian perspective.

SUPERPOWERS

You're a vehement defender of what's best for humanity.
Aquarius is associated with the Eleventh House of Friendships,
so you tend to prioritize concepts and causes that benefit society
as a whole versus the individual. From climate change to an
issue affecting your neighborhood, you speak up and practice
what you preach to make a difference—and, in turn, make an
impression on others.

You're an innovator. Because you're not only unafraid to strike
out on your own but also take great pleasure in it, you're innately
inventive and likely the trendsetter of your group of friends and
colleagues.

You can make friends with everyone. Open and amiable, you're
up for chatting with just about anyone, and, in turn, end up
creating a diverse tapestry of platonic connections.

CHALLENGES

You're big on shock value. You have a habit of declaring a belief
or bringing up an out-there idea simply to rile people up and spur
a debate, which, sure, might make for interesting conversation,
but can also lead to unnecessary conflict.

You often fall into all-or-nothing thinking patterns. Your difficulty
with accepting nuance and insistence that an idea is entirely
wrong or right can lead to friction.

You refuse to back down. In your desire to be different and true to yourself, you might dig your heels in to the point that you reach a complete impasse with friends, loved ones, or coworkers.

LIKE-MINDED MATCHES

You innately understand people born with Mercury or other big six placements in fellow air signs, breezy Gemini and social butterfly Libra, as both share your high mental energy and appetite for connecting with others. You'll also sync up with free-spirited Sagittarius and independent Aries who are as invested in individuality and making the most of the future as you.

TOUGHER CONNECTIONS

People born with Mercury or other big six placements in proud Leo, your opposite sign, are inclined toward self-focus, which can get under your skin. The other two fixed signs, luxury- and comfort-loving Taurus and intimacy-craving Scorpio, mirror your ability to be resolute but are stubborn about aspects of life that don't interest you in the same way.

Pisces

Y ou're an emotionally perceptive and empathic communicator. People you interact with could be taken aback by or impressed with how well you pick up on their mood or mental state without them saying a word. And you'll often respond in a way that's not necessarily direct either. For instance, if you sense that a friend or loved one needs a little extra TLC, you'll speak more softly, lean in a bit closer, or offer to brew a pot of tea. Intuitive and spiritually minded, you're comfier with concepts and ideas that are abstract, like art, poetry, or daydreams, as opposed to harsh realities, facts, and figures. This is the result of Pisces's modern ruler, Neptune, the planet of imagination that clouds rational thought and influences your mindset. Easily swept up by whatever's in your heart, you might have trouble thinking in a logical way, which can interfere with your ability and desire to make up your mind. While this could be perceived as flighty, you simply want to feel out a situation or see how you respond in the moment.

SUPERPOWERS

You're invested in connecting with others in a way that makes them feel comforted and supported. As a sensitive soul yourself, you know how much it can help to feel heard and seen, so you innately aim to offer that to others.

You're capable of thinking and communicating in a spiritual, even psychic way. You have a special gift of being able to intuit the tone of an environment and the experiences of others around you. Although this can take a toll on your energy, it allows you to hone more advanced mystical skills, such as manifestation or mediumship.

Your imagination is unparalleled. Your idealism, open-mindedness, and Jupiter-fueled optimism make you a wide-eyed, poetic dreamer whose mind drifts toward beautiful ideas that other people might never allow themselves to envision.

CHALLENGES

You might be clouded by rose-colored glasses. Because you prefer to lean into fantasy over reality, you might have trouble teasing out what's real from what's not.

You can be vague and confusing. Whether it's because you're trying not to say something that'll rock the boat or you're simply not sure of how you feel, your indirectness might spur head-scratching from others.

Your heart can skew your perspective. Because you see the world through your emotions first and you're frequently trying to tease out how others are feeling, you may have a rough time engaging with the present moment.

LIKE-MINDED MATCHES

People born with Mercury or other big six placements in fellow water signs, caring Cancer and intense Scorpio, understand just how much emotions color your point of view. You may also hit it off with a calm, sensual Taurus or a down-to-earth, goal-oriented Capricorn who can help ground you.

TOUGHER CONNECTIONS

You might find it stressful interacting with people whose Mercury or other big six placements are in analytical Virgo, your opposite sign, because they're so devoted to routine, rationality, and minute, factual details. The other mutable signs, information-seeking Gemini and unfiltered Sagittarius, possess priorities and energies that don't usually harmonize with your own.

Mercury Sign Compatibility

Use this chart to get a sense of how you'll hit it off (or potentially clash) with a friend, loved one, partner, or colleague by matching their Mercury sign and yours.

KEY

For more info on the text below, see The Aspects on page 19.

Conjunction: You're in sync in terms of how you gather and share information. Having so much in common can promote understanding but also fuel eye rolls spurred by an overload of the same energy.

Opposition: Because you communicate in opposing ways, you can join forces to become a formidable team—as long as you hold space for your contrasting views.

Quincunx: Without the same element or modality, your communication styles and points of view are quite different, which is a case for seeking out opportunities to learn from one another.

Trine: Because your Mercury signs are in the same element, your mental connection is naturally harmonious, making for innately enjoyable conversation and collaboration.

Square: You share the same modality but not the same element, leading to different mindsets, amplified tension, and sometimes frustration. If you're able to lean into one another's strengths, this dynamic can be productive.

Sextile: Your Mercury signs are in compatible elements, which means you share an easygoing, intellectual bond that allows you to get on the same page.

Semi-sextile: Because you don't share the same element or modality, you'll likely have to put in extra work to "get" one another. But because you have such different approaches to self-expression, there's much you can learn from each other.

	Aries	Taurus
Aries	Conjunction	Semi-sextile
Taurus	Semi-sextile	Conjunction
Gemini	Sextile	Semi-sextile
Cancer	Square	Sextile
Leo	Trine	Square
Virgo	Quincunx	Trine
Libra	Opposition	Quincunx
Scorpio	Quincunx	Opposition
Sagittarius	Trine	Quincunx
Capricorn	Square	Trine
Aquarius	Sextile	Square
Pisces	Semi-sextile	Sextile

Gemini	Cancer	Leo	Virgo	Libra	Scorpio	Sagittarius	Capricorn	Aquarius	Pisces

PART FOUR

All About Your Mercury House Placement

Now that you know more about your natal Mercury, you can go one step further and consider your Mercury sign's house placement. This piece of the puzzle is much easier to explore than it might seem, and because it can offer another layer of intel on how your Mercury flaunts its powers in your everyday life, it is well worth diving into.

Imagine each house is like a different stage backdrop in the play of your life. By identifying the house Mercury was moving through when you were born—aka your Mercury house placement—you'll gain more context about who you are as a communicator because you can identify the "scenes," or areas, of your life in which communication is a focus and a strength. To find your Mercury house placement, run your natal chart (see page 12). Locate the Mercury symbol (☿) and check the number noting the house, generally located on the inside of the "slice." For example, if you have Mercury in your second house of income, this means you might do well to apply your writing or public speaking skills to moneymaking. If it's in your eighth house of intimacy, you're not only comfortable with but also deeply curious about heavy topics like sex and death, which could inspire you to prioritize your own spiritual well-being or undertake creative projects that explore these subjects.

Once you know your Mercury house placement, consider it alongside your Mercury sign to get an even more nuanced, insightful perspective on your self-expression. Say your Mercury is in Gemini, which is very inquisitive and social, and it was in the Seventh House of Partnership when you were born. That means you're curious and quick-witted—aka Gemini-like—in one-on-one conversations and collaborations. Or perhaps your Mercury is in Capricorn, which is highly assiduous and practical, and it's in the Eleventh House of Friendships in your chart, which will fuel your ability to set and work toward ambitious goals—Capricorn's forte—as part of a team.

Discovering and learning about your Mercury house placement can help you think about how you currently relate to that area of life and ways in which you might be able to make it even more of a focus moving forward. Doing so could lead to you feeling intellectually fulfilled—and successful. As you read on, you'll also learn what you can do to work with and make the most of your unique placement.

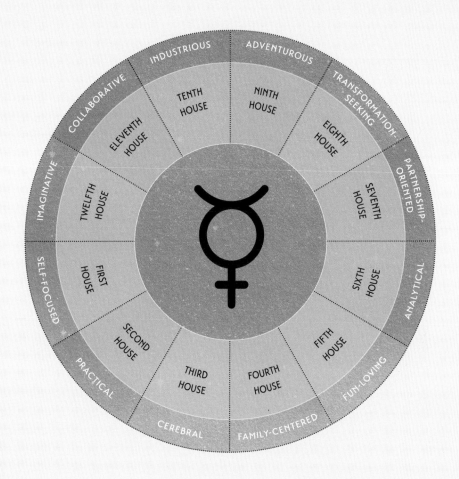

First House of Self

> **Oversees:** Identity, self-image, personality, the physical body, how you deal with uncharted territory, beginnings, and how you present yourself and are perceived by others
>
> **Associated planet:** Mars
>
> **Associated sign:** Aries

You're mercurial, restless, witty, adaptive, and talkative. You're constantly seeking new, mentally stimulating information and are eager to share your discoveries with others.

You come off as a highly curious and open-minded supercommunicator, often presenting your thoughts and opinions in a lively, animated, and perhaps even scattered way. You pride yourself on being up for anything, changeable, spirited, and capable of picking up and pursuing a new path at a moment's notice.

In turn, you're likely not intimidated by public speaking and might even revel in storytelling on stage. Because Mars, the planet of aggression, is naturally associated with the First House of Self and competitive fire sign Aries, you excel as a debater and might find that you enjoy stirring up and engaging in verbal conflicts. You're on a mission to win any and every war of words. In fact, you might struggle to fully listen to and engage with people because you're so focused on your next "move," as if conversations are a game of chess.

Harness your first house Mercury placement by owning your ability to be a visionary and finding just as much delight in listening to others as you do sharing what's on *your* mind. You'll feel most vital when you pursue work or activities that support your desire to come out on top. You could excel as a publicist, spokesperson, or educator. In your free time, you might have fun debating friends or family about current events or filling your days with travel.

Second House of Income

> **Oversees:** Money in all its forms, from spending and earning to paying down debt and setting up a budget; self-worth; material possessions; contentment; your values; your immediate environment; and your five senses
>
> **Associated planet:** Venus
>
> **Associated sign:** Taurus

Your mind is often buzzing about how you can earn, invest, or save. Security is your main objective, and you excel at leveraging your communication skills to make a living and feathering your nest. You're also adept at negotiating and analyzing financial situations.

Like slow-and-steady Taurus, the sign associated with the Second House, you're perfectly happy taking all the time in the world to ponder and strategize, particularly when it comes to pursuing a business deal or networking opportunity. You're quite logical, grounded, and pragmatic. (If your Mercury happens to be in a sign that's anything but rational, like mystical Pisces, you can parlay your imaginative thinking and dreamy communication style into a practical payoff, like writing—and selling—a screenplay or poetry.)

Because you're so aware of your immediate environment and tend to use all five senses when interacting with others, you have a unique ability to synthesize what's going on between the lines and problem solve. When others lack that skill, you could get a bit frustrated. You might also engage in stubborn, fixed ways of thinking, sure that sticking to a hard-and-fast rule or go-to approach will bolster your security.

Take advantage of your second house Mercury placement by putting your wit to work for you and applying it to your dream of building a cozy, stable life while simultaneously striving to be more open-minded. You'll be fulfilled by work that taps into your drive to take a concept and make it concrete, like interior design, wedding planning, or editing. When you're not hammering away at your professional goals, you may enjoy antiquing, redecorating your home, or practicing mindfulness in nature.

Third House of Communication

Oversees: Mental energy; intellect; how you communicate (through writing and speaking), interact with others, and process information; siblings; neighbors; short-distance travel; and learning

Associated planet: Mercury

Associated sign: Gemini

You're an adept conversationalist and information gatherer who excels at socializing and multitasking. Chances are you rely heavily on these skills in your career, which might involve fast-paced technology and frequent travel. You also shine when teaching others, giving presentations or speeches, and staying on top of trending topics.

When it comes to both your professional and personal lives, you don't mind being spread thin and overbooked because you have many interests. It would be almost impossible for you to commit to just one line of work, a couple of hobbies, or a weekend routine. But your intense curiosity and restlessness cause you to run the risk of bailing on an experience or learning opportunity before you've had the chance to absorb enough information.

Make the most of your third house Mercury placement by owning your desire to learn a little bit about a lot, mentoring others, identifying opportunities to express yourself through the written word, and finding ways to get out of your head and into your body (think tai chi or alternate nostril breathing) when your mental energy has been running especially high. You may be drawn to a career path that provides near-perpetual intellectual stimulation, involves short-distance trips, and satiates your boundless curiosity, like working in journalism, public relations, or social media.

Fourth House of Home Life

> **Oversees:** Family and where you nest, your inner life, security, roots, genealogy, what you need to feel like you belong, how you nurture, and how you want to be nurtured
>
> **Associated planet:** The moon
>
> **Associated sign:** Cancer

You find that studying, researching, and learning make you feel more comfortable and secure. You also thrive when engaging in intellectual debate and lively conversation with loved ones.

Given Mercury's restless nature, its presence in your fourth house could mean you move a lot or like to create a sense of home on the go. Maybe you enjoy taking frequent road trips or traveling abroad for weeks on end.

Because your emotions tend to color your mindset and self-expression more than most people, you're artistically inclined but might find it challenging to tap into objective thinking.

The Fourth House encompasses comfort, stability, and tradition—all themes that play into how you think and communicate. Maybe you take great pride in the fact that for generations, your relatives have been praised for having a cheeky sense of humor, so you're especially thrilled by your ability to crack people up. Or perhaps you come from a line of science-minded innovators, so you're often striving to break new ground in your work. No matter what your family history looks like, you value reflecting on your roots and considering how they color your perspective, aspirations, and self-expression.

Own your fourth house Mercury placement by exploring and analyzing your preferences, dislikes, patterns, strengths, and challenges, which can help you better understand how your early life and family contributed to your inner self and emotional well-being. You'll enjoy pastimes like researching your ancestry or serving as the chief documentarian in your family. You could find you're most content when you're able to work from home, perhaps in the field of education or psychology.

Fifth House of Romance and Self-Expression

Oversees: How you own and share your voice with the world, create joy, experience pleasure, interact with children, and have fun, plus flirtation, dating, and the early honeymoon period in a romantic bond

Associated planet: The sun

Associated sign: Leo

You're playful, upbeat, and artistic. Applying your cerebral energy to creative endeavors brings you a great deal of happiness. You're most eager to learn and soak up new information when you're able to have fun doing so. For instance, if you're figuring out how to best navigate a new project alongside colleagues, you'd enjoy brainstorming strategies by playing a game.

Because the Fifth House is dedicated to the beginning phase of heartfelt relationships, chances are you excel at meeting new people, fostering rapport on first dates, and prioritizing lively, engaging, humorous conversation with a significant other. You're a natural at regaling others with your vivacious storytelling skills, and friends and colleagues often rely on you to take the lead because you have a way of upping the entertainment—and sometimes, the drama—factor that makes even a routine meeting more fun.

You can apply your fifth house Mercury placement by sharing your wisdom with others in high-spirited, uplifting ways and striving to empower others—especially children or those younger than you—with your signature buoyant spirit. Your ideal occupation allows for lots of self-expression and offers plenty of opportunities to step into the spotlight. For instance, you may enjoy working in entertainment (like screenwriting), childcare, or arts education, as you could very well become the professor students are eager to take a course with. Creative, whimsical pastimes, from starring in a local theater production to taking painting or dance classes, appeal the most.

Sixth House of Daily Routine and Wellness

Oversees: Details of everyday life and health, day-to-day work, self-improvement, pets, nutrition, how you approach being of service to others, and organization

Associated planet: Mercury

Associated sign: Virgo

A natural multitasker, you appreciate having a wide variety of pragmatic tasks on your agenda at any given time. You're capable of sorting out all the specifics of a plethora of projects and getting your ducks in a row quickly and efficiently. You're analytical, diligent, and hardworking, often setting practical goals and seeing them through one step at a time. You also want to be of service to others, gathering and offering up information that your nearest and dearest will find useful.

Your innate attention to detail could veer a bit too far toward the overly critical, perfectionistic, and worrisome at times, so it's crucial to find grounding practices that help you get centered mentally, which also extends to feeling well emotionally and physically. The good news is that because you prioritize your overall well-being, you likely already have a go-to meditation app or regular strength training class.

Take advantage of your sixth house Mercury by celebrating your attention to detail. There's overlooked magic in meticulousness: It's impossible to reach a long-term goal without being thoughtful about all the steps it will take to get there. Still, given your tendency to become a bit consumed with the minutiae of everyday life, do your best to also keep the bigger picture in mind. You could find a great deal of satisfaction working as a professional organizer, personal trainer, or nurse practitioner, and when you're off the clock, you may be happiest when keeping up with healthy self-care routines, writing in a bullet journal, or listening to wellness or self-help audiobooks.

Seventh House of Partnership

Oversees: One-on-one relationships of all kinds—romantic relationships, platonic bonds, professional connections—plus companionship, negotiation, marriage, and mediation

Associated planet: Venus

Associated sign: Libra

With Mercury in the Seventh House, you're innately partnership-oriented, preferring to pair up in social or work situations. You thrive—and think best—when you're participating as part of a pair in a lively tête-à-tête. For instance, you're better able to pinpoint your thoughts on a particular subject by talking it through with a significant other, friend, or business partner. At the same time, coming to a hard-and-fast conclusion isn't exactly your forte. Like the Scales—the symbol of Libra—you value balance so deeply that you may struggle to take a stand. You want to give equal airtime and consideration to all sides of an issue.

You need romantic, platonic, or professional companions who are equally fired up to swap ideas and potentially even get into a passionate debate. You're also likely to desire an SO who is mercurial in nature—maybe they're a teacher, writer, researcher, or lawyer.

Utilize your seventh house Mercury placement by channeling your appetite for paired-up interaction into working with a therapist or mentor. Not only will this benefit your sense of self but it will also strengthen your relationships. You may even be inspired to pursue a career as a couples counselor, mediator, or spokesperson, given your penchant for partnership. You'll do well to devote plenty of time to one-on-one bonding with your nearest and dearest. Engaging in intellectually stimulating pastimes with someone else, like checking out a documentary together or reading the same book, may bring you a lot of joy.

Eighth House of Intimacy and Joint Resources

Oversees: Sex, emotional bonds, the income you share with others (be that a significant other, loved one, family, etc.), transformation, death and rebirth, and inheritances

Associated planet: Pluto

Associated sign: Scorpio

With the messenger planet in your eighth house, you prefer to connect with others on a deep, meaningful level and foster emotionally complex, intimate bonds. You're eager to uncover secrets, solve mysteries, and touch on topics that other people might consider off-limits or taboo—for example, sex. And you'll rarely be okay with just scratching the surface when you're engaged in conversation. You strive to understand and analyze what excites and drives others.

The Plutonian vibe of this placement makes it a truly powerful one, so if and when you want to take center stage, you can be commanding, authoritative, and captivating. Even if you don't work in sales, you can be quite persuasive in part because you're able to apply your intuition to reading between the lines and deciphering what you need to say to convince someone to make a move. You also possess shrewdness around finances and are capable of becoming a savvy investor.

Embrace your eighth house Mercury placement by pursuing work or hobbies that tap into your investigative talents, comfort with intimacy, and exceptional intuitive abilities. For instance, you could be a successful sex therapist, reporter, or lawyer. In your free time, you may enjoy listening to mystery podcasts, following an ongoing dramatic news story, doing couples yoga, or practicing mediumship.

Ninth House of Adventure and Higher Learning

Oversees: Long-distance travel, education, philosophy, personal beliefs, languages and cultures, publishing, truth, and morals

Associated planet: Jupiter

Associated sign: Sagittarius

You're on a perpetual mission to pursue horizon-broadening experiences, whether you're jetting around the world or becoming an officiant for a friend's wedding. You want to take advantage of any and all opportunities to study unfamiliar subjects and hone new skill sets. You think and communicate with the big picture in mind as opposed to dwelling on minutiae or getting in the weeds of a topic. And because you're particularly adept at taking the wisdom you've acquired and applying it to problem solving, friends, loved ones, and colleagues can count on you to tackle challenges with ease.

Philosophical and intrigued by ethics and morals, you're especially motivated to learn about and champion what you see as the truth. You're also not shy about giving bold advice and sharing your opinions in a straightforward—and at times stunningly blunt—way because you value honesty above all else.

Make the most of your ninth house Mercury placement by leaning into being not only an enthusiastic student but also an educator. Your spirited thirst for exploration is inspiring to others, and you have a unique ability to grasp and discuss broad concepts like religion, philosophy, and spirituality. Constantly satiating your appetite for learning is integral to feeling fulfilled mentally and emotionally. Prioritizing globe-trotting adventures, advancing your education, and perhaps even picking up a second or third language in your free time may benefit your mind and spirit. Tap into your innate wanderlust by taking a job that encourages you to pursue travel and eye-opening experiences.

Tenth House of Public Image and Career

Oversees: Your professional path, reputation, authority, material success, father figures, bosses, and achievement

Associated planet: Saturn

Associated sign: Capricorn

Y ou have the ability to use an authoritative communication style to achieve professional success. While you might not seek out the spotlight as a rule, you can capture the attention of those around you with your coolheaded, pragmatic, commanding nature. No matter your position at work, you're comfortable leading the charge on communication-heavy projects (like giving high-pressure presentations) and you excel at interacting with higher-ups. Your underlying motivation is to achieve recognition—and possibly even status—for your industriousness. You're intrinsically ambitious and action-oriented, and you have the ability to persevere in the face of adversity in your career. In fact, you might welcome an uphill battle because you appreciate the challenge!

Mercury's presence in your tenth house could also influence the way in which you're compelled to make your mark professionally. The cerebral, curious energy of the planet colors your relationship to your career, which might mean you put your nose to the grindstone by traveling, writing, researching, teaching, or speaking publicly. You might even be more likely to switch up careers every now and then as a result of being restless.

Take advantage of your tenth house Mercury placement by continuing to set ambitious goals and also taking the time to celebrate your wins along the way. As a born leader, own your ability to command the spotlight and motivate others when you take the stage. While you could be drawn to hobbies that are career adjacent, like being a professional coach or creating social media content that supports your business, you'll also do well to carve out time for non-work-related pastimes, like producing your own podcast or getting lost in books, films, or shows that explore leadership, power, and public image.

Eleventh House of Friendships and Long-Term Aspirations

Oversees: Friendships, acquaintances, group activities, community, organizations, and humanitarian pursuits as well as your long-term hopes and wishes related to your life's purpose

Associated planet: Uranus

Associated sign: Aquarius

You're a community-minded team player. Your platonic and collegial bonds are of utmost importance to you, and you're at your most joyful when you can contribute ideas to a group effort. Though you're perfectly happy to socialize one-on-one, you prefer to be surrounded by your people, whether that's best friends you've had since you were a kid, close colleagues, or fellow members of an organization you enjoy being involved with. Deeply humanitarian, you're compelled to apply your Mercury-powered skills to improving the world. For example, you might use your social media to raise money for a nonprofit you support or canvass for a ballot initiative you want to see passed.

Given Mercury's presence in a house that's associated with Uranus, the planet of revolution, you're forward-thinking, rebellious, and intellectually stimulated by interactions with others. These mental connections could inspire innovative ideas and ambitious aspirations. Though you're generally rational, you often indulge in fantasies that are representative of lofty wishes for your future. For example, you may muse about inventions you'd like to patent or helping lawmakers pass future-minded legislation.

Harness the power of your eleventh house Mercury placement by recognizing your need for connection and community and prioritizing platonic and professional relationships. Feeling like part of a team or merely something bigger than yourself benefits your well-being. In turn, you may want to serve as a member of your city council, work for a nonprofit, or run the social media or community-building arm of a company that's invested in the greater good. In your free time, you may enjoy playing on a recreational athletic team or volunteering for a local charity.

Twelfth House of Spirituality

Oversees: What lies beneath the surface, such as dreams, mysticism, karma, endings, and the unconscious

Associated planet: Neptune

Associated sign: Pisces

You're intensely intuitive and possibly a bit psychic. Whether you'll admit it outwardly or not, you're likely fascinated with the metaphysical world, spirituality, and all things ethereal. You're a vivid dreamer with an incredibly active imagination. You're also sensitive to the energy around you, especially when interacting with others. You pick up on what people *aren't* saying just as much as what they are. And because you interact with people in a compassionate and empathetic way, it's important for you to prioritize self-care and be sure you're differentiating your own thoughts and feelings from those of others. With analytical Mercury in the house of the unconscious, you might be your own worst critic, so cultivating self-compassion is crucial, too.

Because this is an especially secretive, private placement for Mercury, you might struggle to open up and share what's on your mind. Whether you're in a frustrated, sensitive, or aloof headspace, you'll feel most balanced and centered by exploring the root cause of your emotions—potentially through therapy or other psychological or spiritual studies.

Make the most of your twelfth house Mercury placement by tapping into your highly developed imagination. Allow yourself plenty of time and space for letting your mind wander and tuning in to your artistic impulses, whether that's making music, writing poetry, or creating your own yoga flows. You could be deeply satisfied working in a behind-the-scenes capacity as a researcher, academic, librarian, agent for an artist, astrologer, or life coach. Trust in your ability to heal yourself—and others, too. Your wildest dreams could actually be brilliant solutions to your own or loved ones' conundrums.

A CLOSING NOTE

As you've come to learn while reading this book, understanding both your natal Mercury and transiting Mercury can empower you to speak from the heart, share your truth, pursue a particular passion, or scout uncharted territory, literally or intellectually. Although no one celestial body deserves all the credit for everyday events and exciting milestones in your life, Mercury is the one that supports you the most when it comes to finding and owning your voice. Talk about a relationship worth investing in.

It's also a relationship that you'll do well to continue to explore and nurture. Take note of the type of travel that brings you the most joy (maybe hitting the road, as opposed to globe-trotting, is your jam). Prioritize pastimes with friends and loved ones that you find mentally stimulating, whether that's playing a board game, going to the theater, or joining a book club. Be proud of your innate communication style while trying to express yourself and think in ways that might not come as naturally. And meet both your Mercury-fueled strengths and challenges with more self-awareness and compassion.

If you want to advance your astrological skill set and learn more about your natal Mercury, you can work with a professional astrologer or use pro software (see pages 164–165) to learn about the connections (aka aspects) your Mercury makes to other planets, angles, and significant points in your birth chart. You can use the same resources to track transits that activate your Mercury.

You might also investigate your current or next Mercury return, an annual event during which transiting Mercury returns to the exact sign and degrees as your natal Mercury. Your Mercury return chart will offer insight into how you'll communicate and learn for the next year. You can also see if there are any new or full moons—or better yet, lunar or solar eclipses—that are happening in the same sign (or opposite sign) and within 5 degrees or so of your natal Mercury, as these moments could signify the beginning or end of a particular cycle related to your communication and mindset. You may also benefit from keeping an eye on transiting Mercury as it moves through your chart. For instance, you'll know that while it's moving through your seventh house of partnership, one-on-one collaboration could lead to fulfilling opportunities.

If you'd prefer to focus on applying the celestial knowledge you've already learned, that's okay, too. Ultimately, it is my hope that this book has left you feeling inspired to celebrate how your natal Mercury informs your unique self-expression and viewpoint and fired up to take on whatever successes and surprises that transiting Mercury, whether direct or retrograde, may bring. By harnessing the power of the messenger planet, you'll feel even more self-assured in your ability to bring your most whimsical dreams and boldest ideas into being—and that's nothing short of magical.

RESOURCES

If you're interested in learning more about Mercury and/or astrology in general, the following resources can be helpful and informative. These are my favorite books, websites, apps, podcasts, and other educational tools.

Books

* *Raising Baby by the Stars: A New Parent's Guide to Astrology* by Maressa Brown

* *The Essential Guide to Practical Astrology: Everything from Zodiac Signs to Prediction, Made Easy and Entertaining* by April Elliott Kent

* *Astrological Transits: The Beginner's Guide to Using Planetary Cycles to Plan and Predict Your Day, Week, Year (or Destiny)* by April Elliott Kent

* *Planets in Transit: Life Cycles for Living* by Robert Hand

* *Modern Day Magic: 8 Simple Rules to Realize Your Power and Shape Your Life* by Rachel Lang

* *Llewellyn's Daily Planetary Guide: Complete Astrology At-A-Glance* (released annually)

Websites & Apps

* My site, maressabrown.com. Calculate birth charts, use my Mercury sign calculator, and access my recent articles on horoscopes/astrology and lifestyle topics.

* Astrodienst (astro.com). Here you can cast a range of astrology charts and purchase accompanying reports.

* Astro Gold (macOS) or Solar Fire (PC). Professional astrologers generally use either (or both) of these software programs to run charts. Both programs offer brief interpretations of placements.

* Big Sky Astrology (bigskyastrology.com). My mentor April Elliott Kent's website, on which you can read astrology essays and how-tos and order various personalized reports.

* Time Passages (available on iOS and Android). This is the best astrology app for beginners, offering a personal astrology dashboard as well as the ability to run your natal chart, enjoy tailored interpretations of your placements, and access a detailed daily horoscope.

Podcasts

* *Big Sky Astrology Podcast with April Elliott Kent*, hosted by April Elliott Kent

* *Celestial Insights Podcast*, hosted by Celeste Brooks

Working with a
Professional Astrologer

Many people see their astrologer annually to discuss what's coming in the year ahead. Pro tip: Scheduling a reading around your birthday can be especially beneficial because many astrologers will look at your solar return chart, which is based on the specific date and time at which the sun returns to the same spot it was in when you were born. This chart can prepare you for themes, patterns, and opportunities that will pop up over the next twelve months. You can also ask them to run a Mercury return chart.

To book a personal reading, you can visit my website: maressabrown.com. I also recommend working with April Elliott Kent (bigskyastrology.com), Celeste Brooks (astrologybyceleste.com), and Rebecca Gordon (rebeccagordonastrology.com).

No matter who you choose to schedule a session with, you'll do best to find a seasoned astrologer whose background and perspective resonate with you. You may find them via a referral from a friend, your go-to astrology content (such as books, podcasts, or regular forecasts on a website or social media), or through a trusted professional organization like the International Society for Astrological Research (ISAR) or National Council for Geocosmic Research (NCGR).

ACKNOWLEDGMENTS

Writing *Mercury Magic* has been a truly gratifying experience, and my heart is especially full thanks to support from many wonderful friends, loved ones, and colleagues:

Rachael Mt. Pleasant, my upbeat, kind, and always supportive Libra editor whose commitment to balance, beauty, and the details (her Mercury is in Virgo, after all) makes her a woman after my own heart. My publisher, Lia Ronnen, and the talented team at Workman Publishing: Kimberly Ehart, Sarah Smith, Galen Smith, Barbara Peragine, Elissa Santos, Doug Wolff, Chloe Puton, Ilana Gold, Ivanka Perez, Abigail Sokolsky, Megan Nicolay, and Jessica Weil.

My beloved parents, Stuart and Irene, my brother, Elliot, and my sissypants, Emmie, whose natal Mercury (Rx) trines my Mercury, setting the stage for our lively, loving cerebral bond. My aunts Debbie Swanson and Kathy Rubens and cousins Rachel Garcell, Ali Rubens, Merrill Rubens, and Brian Swanson. My honorary aunt Jill Becker Wilson, whose Mercury in intuitive Scorpio fueled her masterful matchmaking skills.

My therapist, Peggy Matson, who frequently guides me to feeling more centered and empowered to pursue my dreams through calm, nurturing, Cancerian communication.

My mentor and technical editor, April Elliott Kent, whose cheerful Leo enthusiasm I truly treasure.

My best friend, Colleen Clohessy, whose grounded and wise Capricornian Venus trines my Mercury, making for nearly thirty years of mutual adoration and deeply fulfilling friendship that I am forever grateful for.

Cherished friends who show up for me time and again, making me feel incredibly lucky and loved: Andrew Kudla, Lisa Crilley, Joann Wolferman, Caitlin Devan, Dion Lim, Meredith Zimnik, Stacey and Jesse Lubin, Amber,

Dan, Gillian, and Nathaniel Levitch, Darby McCullough, Julia Dennison, Elise Ramsbottom, Stephanie Simpson, Briana Lynch-Haddad, Keith White, Becky Gross, and Caitlin Westlake Jaksha.

My dear friend Sheri Reed, whose Scorpionic perspective brings much-appreciated dynamism to everything I'm fortunate enough to team up with her on. And the fantastic team at Care.com, who I am so filled with gratitude for always having my back (Nancy Bushkin, Olivia Petzy, Mike Davis, Mackenzie Nintzel, Jamie Gentges, Natasha Fellion, Aliana Acevedo, Anja Borngaesser, Ashley Austrew, and Nicole Fabian-Weber).

My brilliant wellness/fertility team: Jennifer Shulman, DAOM, L.Ac., Dr. Carolyn Alexander, and Dr. Anupama Kathiresan.

My amazingly generous editors/friends at the publications I contribute to (especially Melissa Bykofsky, Erin Donnelly, Julia Sullivan, Brie Dyas, and the teams at *Parents* and PopSugar.com), who I am endlessly appreciative of. Fellow Mercury in Virgo and publicist Laura Rossi, who I cannot thank enough for just getting *it*—and me. My always patient and lovely social media manager, Mia Festenstein. And the sweetest little writing buddy, Rhiannon aka Annie.

Fellow astrologers whose commitment to sharing proactive, pragmatic wisdom with the world is applause-worthy: KJ Atlas, Celeste Brooks, and Rachel Lang.

Most of all, thank you with all of my heart to my love, my husband, Kyle, whose Mercury in Cancer (conjunct Jupiter!) colors his vivacious, gloriously hilarious and entertaining, and perpetually warmhearted communication style. The way in which you truly listen and express your incredibly caring, emotionally intelligent perspective is an absolute gift to everyone in your life. And because I have the honor of being your wife, I can say I know what it means to feel heard, understood, and truly loved. I love you, I love you.

INDEX

A

adventure, 152–153
  air element, 17
Aquarius
  Mercury in, 82–84
  personality and, 124–126
Aries
  Mercury in, 52–54
  personality and, 94–96
aspects, 19
aspirations, long-term, 156–157

B

birth charts, 12–15

C

Cancer
  Mercury in, 61–63
  personality and, 103–105
Capricorn
  Mercury in, 79–81
  personality and, 121–123
cardinal quality, 18
career, 154–155
casting of birth charts, 13–15
communication, 140–141
compatibility, signs and, 130–131
conjunctions, 19

D

daily routine, 146–147

E

earth element, 17
education, 152–153
eighth house of intimacy and joint resources, 150–151
elements, 17
eleventh house of friendships and long-term aspirations, 156–157
empowerment, 48–49

F

fifth house of romance and self-expression, 144–145
finances, 138–139
fire element, 17
first house of self, 136–137
fixed quality, 18
fourth house of home life, 142–143
friendships, 156–157

G

Gemini
  Mercury in, 58–60
  personality and, 100–102

H

health, 146–147
  Mercury retrograde and, 45–47

higher learning, 152–153
horoscope, Mercury retrograde and, 88–89
house and home life, 142–143
the houses, 20–21
  Mercury and, 132–159

I

image, public, 154–155
income, 138–139
intimacy, 150–151

J

joint resources, 150–151
Jupiter, influence of, 8

L

leadership, 154–155
learning and education, 152–153
Leo
  Mercury in, 64–66
  personality and, 106–108
Libra
  Mercury in, 70–72
  personality and, 112–114
long-term aspirations, 156–157
love, Mercury retrograde and, 37–47
luminaries, 6–7

M

Mars, influence of, 8
Mercury
   and the ecliptic, 27
   essential facts, 26
   influence of, 8
   personality and, 90–131
Mercury retrograde
   effects of, 33–36
   and empowerment, 48–49
   and health, 45–47
   horoscope and, 88–89
   intensity of, 32
   love and, 37–47
   and relationships, 41–44
   work and, 39–41
Moon, influence of, 7
mutable quality, 18

N

natal, versus transmitting, 11
Neptune, influence of, 9
ninth house of adventure
   and higher learning,
   152–153

O

opposition, 19

P

partnership, 148–149
personality, Mercury and,
   90–131
Pisces
   Mercury in, 85–87
   personality and, 127–129
planets, 6–9
   ruling, 16
   as signs, 10–11

Pluto, influence of, 9
post-shadows, 30–31
pre-shadows, 30–31
professions, 154–155
public image, 154–155

Q

qualities, 18
quincunx, 19

R

relationships, Mercury
   retrograde and, 41–44
resources, joint, 150–151
retrograde, 28–36
   intense days of, 32
   planets and, 29
romance, 37–47, 144–145
routine, 146–147
ruling planets, 16

S

Sagittarius
   Mercury in, 76–78
   personality and, 118–120
Saturn, influence of, 9
Scorpio
   Mercury in, 73–75
   personality and, 115–117
second house of income,
   138–139
self-expression, 144–145
self-identity, 136–137
semi-sextile, 19
seventh house of
   partnership, 148–149
sextile, 19
sign seasons, 50–89
signs, meaning of, 10–11

sixth house of daily routine
   and wellness, 146–147
spirituality, 158–159
square, 19
storm periods, 32
Sun, influence of, 7

T

Taurus
   Mercury in, 55–57
   personality and, 97–99
tenth house of public image
   and career, 154–155
third house of
   communication,
   140–141
transmitting, versus natal, 11
trine, 19
twelfth house of spirituality,
   158–159

U

Uranus, influence of, 9

V

Venus, influence of, 8
Virgo
   Mercury in, 67–69
   personality and, 109–111

W

water element, 17
wellness, 146–147
   Mercury retrograde and,
   45–47
work, Mercury retrograde
   and, 39–41

ABOUT THE AUTHOR

MARESSA BROWN is an author, journalist, and astrologer who has written parenting, astrology, pop culture, and general lifestyle content for nearly two decades. She is the author of *Raising Baby by the Stars: A New Parent's Guide to Astrology* (Artisan, 2023) and senior editor for Care.com, and she has served as resident astrologer for various publications, such as *InStyle* and *Shape*. Her writing has also appeared in *Parents* magazine, Yahoo Life, *SELF*, the *Washington Post*, PopSugar.com, Horoscope.com, Astrology.com, and more. A graduate of Emerson College, Brown is a member of the International Society for Astrological Research, the American Society of Journalists and Authors, and the Authors Guild. She lives in Los Angeles. You can find more about her work at maressabrown.com.